# Foundation Physics

## Keith Gibbs and Robert Hutchings

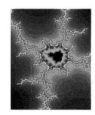

Series editor
**Fred Webber**

Consultant editors
**John Raffan**
**Michael Reiss**

CAMBRIDGE
UNIVERSITY PRESS

Published by the Press Syndicate of the University of Cambridge
The Pitt Building, Trumpington Street, Cambridge CB2 1RP
40 West 20th Street, New York, NY 10011-4211, USA
10 Stamford Road, Oakleigh, Melbourne 3166, Australia

First published 1995

Printed in Great Britain at the University Press, Cambridge

A catalogue record for this book is available from the British
Library

ISBN 0 521 42197 7 paperback

Designed and produced by Gecko Ltd, Bicester, Oxon

This book is one of a series produced to support individual
modules within the Cambridge Modular Sciences scheme.
Teachers should note that written examinations will be set
on the content of each module as defined in the syllabus.
This book is the authors' interpretation of the module.

Front cover photograph: Fractal geometry from within the
Mandelbrot set; Gregory Sams/Science Photo Library

# Contents

# Acknowledgements

1, Tony Hallas/Science Photo Library; 2, Courtesy of Bureau International des Poids et Mesures, Sèvres, Paris, France; 3*tl*, 23, 29, 30*t*, NASA/ Science Photo Library; 3*tr*, *bl*, 11*t*, 18, 33*b*, 35*t*, 43, 48, 73*t*, *b*, Tick Ahearn; 3*br*, Philippe Plailly/ Science Photo Library; 5, Ronald Sheridan/Ancient Art and Architecture Collection; 7, Dr Mitsuo Ohtsuki/Science Photo Library; 8, 15, 20*r*, 27*r*, 38*t*, 42, Images Colour Library; 9, 16*l*, Colorsport; 10, Abbie Enock/Life File; 11*b*, Alan Lockyer/Somerset News (NAPA); 14*t*, S. Jonasson/ FLPA; 14*b*, Paul Richards/Life File; 16*r*, Gray Mortimore/Allsport; 20*tl*, Didier Klein/ Vandystadt/Allsport; 20*bl*, Simon Ward/Allsport; 21, Allsport; 26, 57*r*, 59*tl*, *bl*, Michael Brooke; 27*l*, Bernard Giani/Vandystadt/Allsport; 28*t*, Howard Boylan/Allsport; 28*b*, Prof. Harold Edgerton/Science Photo Library; 30*b*, David Cannon/Allsport; 33*t*, Peter Dunkley/Life File; 35b, Colorsport/De Nombel; 37, 40, Bob Martin/ Allsport; 38*bl*, Victor Kolpakov/TRIP; 38*br*, Nigel Shuttleworth/Life File; 39, NOAO/Science Photo Library; 44, Travel Ink/Life File; 47, Douglas W. Johnson/Science Photo Library; 50*l*, Cliff Threadgold/Life File; 50*r*, David Parker/ Science Photo Library; 52, Michael Freeman/Bruce Coleman; 55*l*, Peter Aprahamian/Science Photo Library; 55*tr*, Jens Meyer/Fotex/Rex Features Ltd; 55*br*, Steve Gillett/Performing Arts Library; 56, 72, Andrew Lambert; 57*l*, Peter Aprahamian/Sharples Stress Engineers Ltd/Science Photo Library; 59*r*, The Natural History Museum, London; 63*t*, Will and Deni McIntyre/Science Photo Library; 63*b*, John Greim/Science Photo Library; 65, Travel Ink/Life File; 66, Adam Hart-Davis/Science Photo Library; 69*l*, Graham Portlock; 69*r*, Gordon Garradd/Science Photo Library; 70, Lionel Moss/ Life File; 74, Richard Megna/Fundamental Photos/ Science Photo Library; 78, 79, University of Cambridge, Cavendish Laboratory, Madingley Road, Cambridge, England; 83, Royal Observatory, Edinburgh/AATB/Science Photo Library; 85, Michael Holford

## Chapter one

# Physical quantities and units

1 understand that all physical quantities consist of a numerical magnitude and a unit;

2 recall the base quantities and their units;

3 express derived units in terms of the base units;

4 use the base units to check the homogeneity of equations;

5 understand and use the correct methods for labelling graphs and for setting out table columns;

6 use prefixes and powers of ten when expressing the magnitude of quantities;

7 make reasonable estimates of physical quantities;

8 understand the significance of the Avogadro constant;

9 use molar quantities;

10 distinguish between scalar and vector quantities and give examples;

11 define *displacement*;

12 add and subtract coplanar vectors;

13 represent a vector as two perpendicular components.

## Physical quantities

Physics is the study of the physical world around us. It is a science of measurement. Physicists deal with times from as short as $3.3 \times 10^{-24}$ s (the time for light to cross a proton) up to $1.5 \times 10^{10}$ years (the 'age' of the Universe), distances from $2.5 \times 10^{-15}$ m (the diameter of the nucleus of a hydrogen atom) to $1.4 \times 10^{26}$ m (the distance from the Earth to the most remote quasar known at present) and masses from $3.7 \times 10^{-36}$ kg (the 'mass' of a quantum of yellow light) to over $1 \times 10^{42}$ kg (the mass of the Andromeda galaxy) *(figure 1.1)*. If the notation is unfamiliar, read the box on the right.

Notice that all these physical quantities consist of a *number* and a *unit*, without either of these the measurement is meaningless: a

mass of 60 or a height of centimetres means nothing. You must add kilograms after the 60 and 175 before the centimetres.

### A mathematical note

At advanced level we use a different way of writing powers of ten: for example, one-tenth or 0.1 is written as $10^{-1}$, one-hundredth or 0.01 as $10^{-2}$, a thousand (1000) as $10^3$, a million as $10^6$, and so on. This means that the number 0.0125 can be written as $1.25 \times 10^{-2}$, while 12500 can be written as $1.25 \times 10^4$. It will help you considerably if you can familiarise yourself with this way of writing; it is especially helpful with very large and very small numbers. For example, the charge on one electron is usually written as $-1.602 \times 10^{-19}$ C and not as $-0.000\,000\,000\,000\,000\,000\,160\,2$ C!

### Use of your calculator

Some students have problems with powers of ten and a calculator. Keying in $2.5 \times 10^3$ causes no problems – you should press 2.5 EXP 3. The difficulty seems to come when expressing $10^3$; following the same ideas as before and remembering that it is simply $1 \times 10^3$, you should press 1 EXP 3 and *not* 10 EXP 3 (the latter would give you $10^4$). (Some calculators have an EE key in place of the EXP.)

● *Figure 1.1* A galaxy represents some of the largest quantities in physics. It could be up to $10^{25}$ m away from the Earth and could have a mass of around $10^{42}$ kg.

## Powers of ten

Often, when dealing with very small or very large numbers, it is easier to include the power of ten in the unit, by adding a prefix to the unit. In physics we often deal with such numbers, and it is important to understand how these may be represented *(table 1.1)*.

| atto | (a) | $10^{-18}$ | centi | (c) | $10^{-2}$ |
|------|-----|-----------|-------|-----|-----------|
| femto | (f)* | $10^{-15}$ | deci | (d) | $10^{-1}$ |
| pico | (p) | $10^{-12}$ | kilo | (k) | $10^{3}$ |
| nano | (n) | $10^{-9}$ | mega | (M) | $10^{6}$ |
| micro | (µ) | $10^{-6}$ | giga | (G) | $10^{9}$ |
| milli | (m) | $10^{-3}$ | tera | (T) | $10^{12}$ |

*One femtometre (1fm) is also called a fermi.

● **Table 1.1** Powers of ten

# Units

All units used in this book are based on the Système International (SI) of units. There are seven 'base units' from which all others can be derived. In this book we need to use the following six units – you do not need to learn all the definitions!

### Mass

Mass is measured in kilograms. The **kilogram** (kg) is the mass equal to that of the International Prototype Kilogram kept at the Bureau International des Poids et Mesures at Sèvres, France *(figure 1.2)*.

### Length

Length is measured in metres. The **metre** (m) is the distance travelled by electromagnetic waves in free space in 1/299 792 458 s.

### Time

Time is measured in seconds. The **second** (s) is the duration of 9 192 631 770 periods of the radiation corresponding to the transition between two hyperfine levels of the ground state of the caesium-137 atom.

### Electric current

Electric current is measured in amperes. The **ampere** (A) is that constant current which, if

● **Figure 1.2** The International Prototype Kilogram.

maintained in two parallel straight conductors of infinite length and of negligible circular cross-section placed 1 m apart in a vacuum, would produce a force between them of $2 \times 10^{-7}$ N per metre length.

### Temperature

Temperature is measured in kelvins. The **kelvin** (K) is defined as 1/273.16 of the thermodynamic temperature of the triple point of water. The kelvin has the same numerical size as the degree celsius (°C):

$$\text{temperature/K} = \text{temperature/°C} + 273$$

### Amount of substance

Amount of substance is measured in moles. The **mole** (mol) is the amount of substance of a system that contains as many elementary particles as there are atoms in 0.012 kg of carbon-12.

It is most important to realise that you cannot mix these quantities, i.e. you cannot add metres to kilograms or seconds to moles! It is rather similar to having a small housing estate in which there are 30 houses, 12 cars and 65 people, and asking how many there are. How many of what? It is simply a collection of different things – you cannot add them together!

# Using quantities and units

## *Checking that equations 'balance'*

We can use the base units to check that an equation is correct. Remember the example of the housing estate; it would be meaningless to say 30 houses = 12 cars + 65 people. It is the same with the equations of physics. If mass, length and time appear on one side of an equation, then they must also appear on the other, and to the same power.

Consider the following equation, which you will find explained fully in chapter 2 (page 18):

$$s = ut + \tfrac{1}{2}at^2$$

(where $s$ = displacement, $u$ = initial velocity, $a$ = acceleration, $t$ = time). Writing down the units for each side, we have:

$$\text{m} = \text{ms}^{-1} \times \text{s} + \text{ms}^{-2} \times \text{s}^2 \quad \text{giving} \quad \text{m} = \text{m} + \text{m}$$

Although it may look strange that m = m + m, this is not a contradiction. It means that one length measured in metres is obtained by adding together two other lengths also measured in metres.

Note that we will use $\text{ms}^{-2}$ instead of m/s$^2$ throughout this book; similarly m/s will be written as $\text{ms}^{-1}$ and so on.

## SAQ 1.1

Use the ideas above to check the following equations:

**a**  $m = V\rho$, where $m$ = mass, $V$ = volume, $\rho$ = density.

**b**  $v = u + at^2$, where $v$ = final velocity, $u$ = initial velocity, $a$ = acceleration, $t$ = time.

**c**  $F = mv^2/r$, where $F$ = force, $m$ = mass, $v$ = velocity, $r$ = radius of a circle.

## *Approximate sizes and values*

It is always useful to be able to estimate the size of a quantity (*figure 1.3*), so that when you complete an experiment or suggest a theory you have some idea of what value you might expect. An important phrase here is 'the right order of magnitude' – this means getting the right sort of number; for example, finding $g$ as $9.8\,\text{ms}^{-2}$ and not $980\,\text{ms}^{-2}$, getting the temperature of melting lead to be $330\,°\text{C}$ and not $3300\,°\text{C}$, or working out that the cost of running a

● *Figure 1.3* These objects represent a huge range of sizes, from $10^7\,\text{m}$ (the radius of the Earth) to $10^{-10}\,\text{m}$ (the radius of an atom).

100 W light bulb for 2 h is 2 p and not 200 p. Of course, all these examples would be meaningless without the correct units, so do not forget to put them in.

*Table 1.2* contains a list of some quantities. There are some estimations for you to make in SAQ 1.2.

| | |
|---|---|
| Distance from Earth to most distant quasar known | $1.4 \times 10^{26}\,\text{m}$ |
| Diameter of an atomic nucleus | $10^{-14}\,\text{m}$ |
| Mass of a human | $50\,\text{kg}$–$100\,\text{kg}$ |
| Mass of a car | $1000\,\text{kg}$ |
| Mass of the Earth | $10^{24}\,\text{kg}$ |
| Volume of a human head | $4 \times 10^{-3}\,\text{m}^3$ |
| Resistance of a metre of copper wire | $0.005\,\Omega$ |

● *Table 1.2* Some estimated quantities

## SAQ 1.2

Estimate: **a** the mass of this textbook; **b** the volume of your laboratory;  **c** the volume of a cat; **d** the tension in a stretchy clothes belt; **e** the temperature of a hot bath; **f** the rate of wing beat of a bee (in Hz).

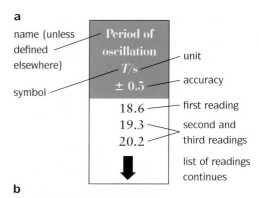

**a**

name (unless defined elsewhere)

symbol

Period of oscillation
*T*/s
± 0.5

unit

accuracy

18.6 — first reading

19.3 — second and
20.2 — third readings

list of readings continues

**b**

| Name of quantity | Symbol/unit |
|---|---|
| Time | $t$/s |
| Frequency | $f$/Hz |
| Length | $l$/m |
| Height | $h$/m |
| Mass | $M$/kg |
| Velocity | $v$/m s$^{-1}$ |
| Acceleration | $a$/m s$^{-2}$ |
| Resistance | $R$/Ω |
| Current | $I$/A |
| Potential difference | $V$/V |

● **Table 1.3** A results table and units

## Tables of results

The presentation of results and units in a results table is of great importance and therefore an example of what it should look like is shown in *table 1.3*. *Table 1.3b* shows how series of quantities and their respective units should be presented. For example, *I*/A means that the current *I* is measured in amperes (A) and *f*/Hz that the frequency *f* is measured in hertz (Hz).

## Drawing a graph

When drawing graphs, the points listed and noted on *figure 1.4* should be remembered.

### SAQ 1.3

The acceleration due to gravity (*g*) can be found using a simple pendulum of length *L* and with a period *T*, for which *T* and *L* are related by the formula $T^2 = 4\pi^2 L/g$. Use the data below to plot a graph of $T^2$ against *L*, and use your graph to determine the acceleration due to gravity. Special care should be taken with the presentation of your work.

| *L*/m | 0.225 | 0.305 | 0.380 | 0.460 | 0.555 | 0.675 | 0.805 | 0.915 |
|---|---|---|---|---|---|---|---|---|
| *T*/s | 0.950 | 1.110 | 1.240 | 1.360 | 1.500 | 1.650 | 1.800 | 1.920 |

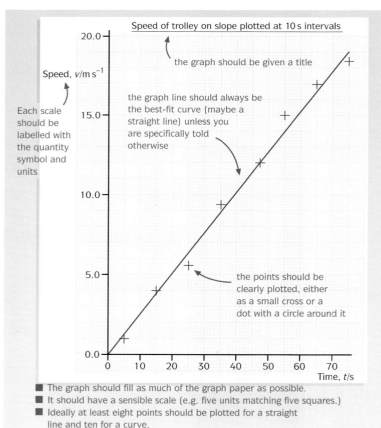

Speed of trolley on slope plotted at 10 s intervals

the graph should be given a title

Speed, *v*/m s$^{-1}$

Each scale should be labelled with the quantity symbol and units

the graph line should always be the best-fit curve (maybe a straight line) unless you are specifically told otherwise

the points should be clearly plotted, either as a small cross or a dot with a circle around it

Time, *t*/s

■ The graph should fill as much of the graph paper as possible.
■ It should have a sensible scale (e.g. five units matching five squares.)
■ Ideally at least eight points should be plotted for a straight line and ten for a curve.

● **Figure 1.4** How to draw a graph.

# Early ideas about atoms and molecules

When you look around, you see a world of well-known objects, people, grass, cars, buildings, etc., but what are they made of? If we could 'cut up' a stone, how far could we go before the particles became indivisible? The first people in the Western world to wonder about the structure of matter were the Greeks *(figure 1.5)*. One of the first ideas was that of Empedocles (484–424 BC), who suggested that all matter was made up of various amounts of four basic 'elements' – Earth, Air, Fire and Water (450 BC). It was Democritus (460–370 BC) who suggested that all matter was made up of indivisible particles and that there were spaces between them. He called these particles 'atoms' – from the Greek word *atomos*. Unfortunately Aristotle (384–332 BC) rejected that idea; and since he was an eminent philosopher, everyone believed him and not

● *Figure 1.5* Remains of the water clock of Andronikos. The Greeks played a large part in the development of science.

Democritus! There was then a gap of many centuries until Gassendi (1592–1655) revived the atomic ideas, suggesting that atoms were massive particles with inertia. Newton expressed Gassendi's ideas almost exactly in his book *Optiks*. The ideas were further expanded by John Dalton, a Quaker weaver and school-teacher in Manchester. He was the founder of the modern atomic theory, based on his work with gases. In 1803 he proposed the theory that there were separate 'ultimate particles' or **atoms,** and that the original 'elements' – Earth, Air, Fire and Water – were made up of many different kinds of these atoms. He called each kind of particle an **element.** He also proposed that all atoms of the same element had the same mass. A group of atoms chemically joined together he called a **molecule.**

## Brownian motion

The first direct evidence for the existence of molecules came from an experiment by the Scottish botanist Robert Brown in 1827. He noticed that tiny pollen grains in water were moving randomly although the water had been left standing for some time. Brown realised that the pollen grains were moving in this random way because they were being bombarded continually from all sides by the much smaller and invisible water molecules. The modern version of this experiment uses a smoke cell *(figure 1.6)*. Smoke is blown into a small glass cell and a microscope is focussed on the cloud. When the smoke is viewed through the microscope, tiny star-like objects can be seen juddering around all over the place. These are the particles of smoke. The smoke particles are much larger than the air molecules, and so they do not move much. Heating the air makes the motion more violent, as the air molecules have gained energy.

## SAQ 1.4

What would you notice in the Brownian motion experiment if larger smoke particles were used? Explain your answer.

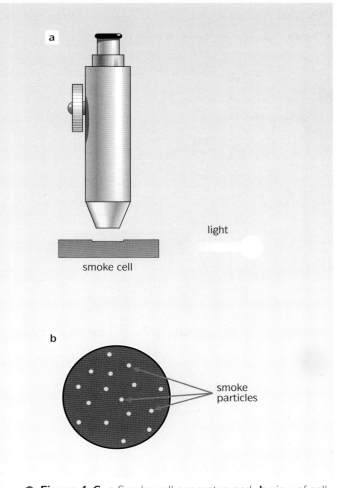

● *Figure 1.6* **a** Smoke cell apparatus and **b** view of cell.

## The size of a molecule

A simple measurement of the size of a molecule was made in 1899 by Lord Rayleigh using the spreading effect of a drop of oil on water. The experiment is described in the box.

---

### Experiment to find the size of a molecule

Get a small oil drop on a fine wire loop and, using a travelling microscope, measure its diameter (2$r$). Take a large flat tray and fill it to the brim with water. Then clean the surface by pulling two waxed rods apart from the centre of the tray *(figure 1.7)*. It may help to see the oil drop if you scatter a fine, coloured powder on the surface of the water. Place the drop of oil onto the water surface (or onto the powder, if you have used it) and measure the diameter of the circle (2$R$) into which the drop spreads. The volume of the liquid drop must equal the volume of the cylinder of liquid on the water surface. Therefore:

$$\tfrac{4}{3}\pi r^3 = \pi R^2 t$$

where $t$ is the thickness of the film. Since the film must be at least one molecule thick, the length of an oil molecule must be no greater than $t$. This simple experiment gives a rough idea of the size of a molecule.

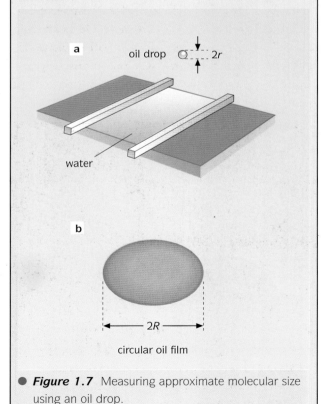

● *Figure 1.7* Measuring approximate molecular size using an oil drop.

---

# The mole, relative atomic mass and the Avogadro constant

Before looking more closely at atoms and molecules, we must look at the units that are used to measure their mass. In physics the basic mass unit is defined in terms of the mass of the carbon-12 atom. This element was chosen because of its relative abundance and the ease with which it could be used.

The mole is the SI unit for the amount of material in a substance. The **mole** is the amount of matter that contains the same number of atoms (or molecules) as there are atoms in 0.012 kg of carbon-12.

The **molar mass** of a substance is the mass of one mole (1 mol) of that substance (units kg mol$^{-1}$).

The **Avogadro constant** is the number of atoms in 0.012 kg of carbon-12. If one carbon-12 atom has a mass of $19.92 \times 10^{-27}$ kg, then in 0.012 kg there are $0.012/(19.92 \times 10^{-27}) = 6.02 \times 10^{23}$ atoms. The Avogadro constant is given the symbol $L$; $L = 6.02 \times 10^{23}$ mol$^{-1}$.

The **relative atomic mass** or **relative molecular mass** is the mass of the atom (or molecule) divided by 1/12 the mass of an atom of carbon-12. The quantity '1/12 the mass of an atom of carbon-12' is sometimes referred to as the *unified atomic mass unit*.

If the substance exists in atomic form, such as iron, then 1 mol (56 g) of iron contains $6.02 \times 10^{23}$ iron *atoms*. If it exists in molecular form, like ammonia ($NH_3$) then 1 mol of ammonia (17 g) contains $6.02 \times 10^{23}$ ammonia *molecules*.

These definitions mean that the following masses of substances contain equal numbers of atoms (or molecules): 2 g of hydrogen ($H_2$), 60 g of cobalt-60 (Co), 18 g of water ($H_2O$), 137 g of caesium-137 (Cs), 24 g of magnesium (Mg), 235 g of uranium-235 (U), 32 g of oxygen ($O_2$) and 63 g of copper (Cu).

We shall now do two examples. The first is to calculate the number of atoms in 0.006 kg of carbon.

From the definitions above, the relative atomic mass of carbon is 12, so 1 mol of carbon has a mass of 0.012 kg. There are $6.02 \times 10^{23}$ atoms in every mole of a substance (the Avogadro constant). In 0.006 kg of carbon there are 0.006/0.012 = 0.5 moles. So there are $0.5 \times 6.02 \times 10^{23}$ = $3.01 \times 10^{23}$ atoms of carbon present.

The second example is to calculate the number of molecules in $200 \, cm^3$ of water.

Density of water = $1000 \, kg\,m^{-3}$ = $1 \, g\,cm^{-3}$. Therefore $200 \, cm^3$ of water has a mass of 0.2 kg. Molecular formula of water is $H_2O$, so the relative molecular mass = $1 \times 2 + 16 = 18$. So 0.018 kg of water contain $6.02 \times 10^{23}$ molecules. Therefore 0.2 kg of water contain $\dfrac{0.2 \times 6.02 \times 10^{23}}{0.018}$

$= 6.69 \times 10^{24}$ molecules

## SAQ 1.5

**a** How many molecules are there in a 1.5 litre jug of water?

**b** How many atoms are there in a small copper coin, mass 5 g?

**c** A research laboratory prepares a sample of very pure magnesium containing $10^{14}$ atoms of magnesium. What is its mass?

**d** A small drop of sulphuric acid (molecular mass 98 g) contains $1.6 \times 10^{19}$ molecules. What is the mass of the drop?

## Measurement of the Avogadro constant

If we know the volume of a mole of atoms of a particular substance and the arrangement of these atoms in a crystal, we can work out the value of the Avogadro constant. The molar mass of copper is 0.063 kg, the density of copper is $8930 \, kg\,m^{-3}$ and therefore the volume of this mass is $7.12 \times 10^{-6} \, m^3$.

We now have to think of the maximum number of atoms that can be fitted into this volume. If we think of them as hard spheres, then *figure 1.8*

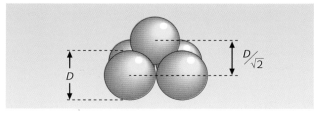

● *Figure 1.8* Arrangement of copper atoms in a crystal.

shows how we would have to stack them to get the most in. The separation of each copper atom is $D$, which is also the atomic diameter of copper. A number of atoms $a/D$ will fit into a length $a$, and a number $b/D$ into a width $b$, so that $ab/D^2$ will fit into a base area $ab$. The next layer is made of atoms nesting in between four of the base atoms. Any one of these has its centre $D/\sqrt{2}$ above the centres of the base layer. The number ($N$) in volume $abc$, where $c$ is the height of several layers, is $N = abc \times \sqrt{2}/D^3$. But the volume ($abc$) for 1 mol is $7.12 \times 10^{-6} \, m^3$. Using X-ray diffraction to find the size of a copper atom gives the diameter $D = 2.55 \times 10^{-10} \, m$, and so the number of atoms in one mole $N = 6.07 \times 10^{23}$, which is approximately equal to the Avogadro constant.

## *How big is an atom?*

Using the numbers earlier in the chapter we can work out that 1 g of water contains $6.02 \times 10^{23}/18$ $= 3.34 \times 10^{22}$ water molecules. However, 1 g of water has a volume of $1 \, cm^3$ and so the average volume of a water molecule must be about $2.99 \times 10^{-23} \, cm^3$ if we ignore any spaces between them. Assuming that the molecules are spherical gives the 'diameter' of a water molecule as about $4 \times 10^{-8} \, cm$, a value confirmed by other methods such as X-ray diffraction. Electron microscopy (*figure 1.9*) can also be used to work out the size of atoms.

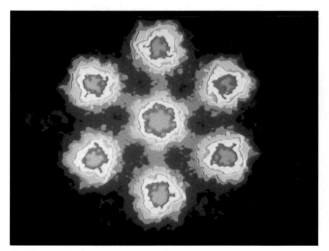

● *Figure 1.9* An electron microscope photograph of uranium atoms in a crystal of uranium ethanoate. How big is each atom?

**SAQ 1.6**

Use the theory above to work out the diameters of the following atoms:

**a** gold – molar mass = 0.197 kg, density = 19 300 kg m$^{-3}$;

**b** aluminium – molar mass = 0.027 kg, density = 2710 kg m$^{-3}$.

# Scalars and vectors

In this chapter so far we have considered atoms and molecules. If we measure how they behave singly or in groups, we have a description of the world around us. These groups of particles may be from the very small, molecular size, to the very large, a galaxy! But so far we have seen only how we can measure numbers of particles and amounts of substances. When we describe how particles and objects move and interact, we need to use quantities that include direction *(figure 1.10)*.

● *Figure 1.10* When objects are moving, it is important to include direction when we measure their movements and when we predict how they might move.

The quantities measured in physics may be divided into two groups: scalars and vectors.

## Scalars

Scalars are quantities that have magnitude (size) only. Examples of scalars are length, speed, mass, density, energy, power, temperature, charge and potential difference.

## Vectors

Vectors are quantities that have direction as well as magnitude, and both must be given when they are used in calculations. Examples of vectors are displacement, force, torque, velocity, acceleration, momentum, electric current and electric field.

Scalars may be added together by simple arithmetic, but when two or more vectors are added together their direction must be taken into account as well. A vector may be represented by a line, the length of the line being the magnitude of the vector and the direction of the line the direction in which it acts. For example, *figure 1.11* shows a force of 20 N acting at 20° to the vertical of the page.

A simple comparison between a vector and a scalar is shown by *figure 1.12*. This shows the distance moved by a referee during a match *(figure 1.13)*. The vector represents the *displacement* between the starting position (A) and the position

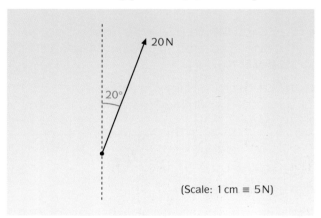

(Scale: 1 cm ≡ 5N)

● *Figure 1.11* Vector representation.

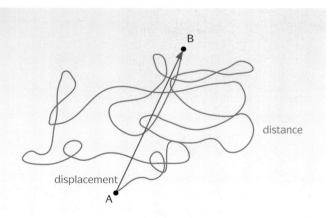

● *Figure 1.12* The movement of a referee during part of a match: distance in blue, displacement in red.

at the end of the game (B), while the wavy line (a scalar) is the *distance* that the referee has actually run during the game (much further!). **Displacement** is defined as the difference between the position of a body at a given time and its initial position.

## *Vector addition*

### Vectors acting at the same point in the same direction

Two or more vectors acting in the same direction may be added as if they were scalars. For example, the sum, or **resultant**, of the two forces shown in *figure 1.14a* is 50 N acting from left to right.

### Vectors acting at the same point in different directions

The triangle of vectors shown in *figure 1.14b* is used to add two vectors that are acting in different directions. The resultant is the vector that closes the triangle. In the example shown, the resultant is 40 N, in the direction shown.

If more than two vectors act at a point, then the polygon of vectors is used. The resultant is now the vector that closes the polygon *(figure 1.15)*.

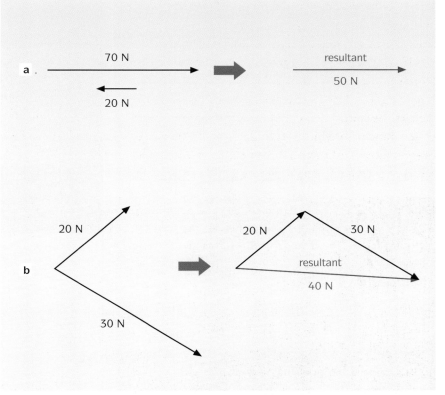

● *Figure 1.14* Vector addition.

● *Figure 1.13* A referee may run many kilometres during a match, but will have little displacement to show for it!

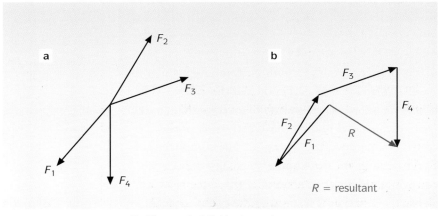

● *Figure 1.15* Vector polygon.

## SAQ 1.7

Copy and complete the following table:

| Vector A /N | Vector B /N | Direction A /degrees | Direction B /degrees | Resultant /N | Resultant direction/degrees |
|---|---|---|---|---|---|
| 10 | 10 | 180 | 90 | | |
| 4 | 8 | 210 | 270 | | |
| 15 | 12 | 30 | 120 | | |
| 6 | 8 | 350 | 190 | | |
| 12 | 15 | 200 | 100 | | |

[The resultants may be calculated using scale diagrams or trigonometry. The angles are taken using the upward vertical as zero and measuring in a clockwise direction. In each case the forces *A* and *B* are coplanar (in the same plane) and act at a single point.]

## SAQ 1.8

Draw a graph showing how the resultant of two equal vectors varies as the angle between them increases from 0° to 360°.

## SAQ 1.9

What is the resultant of the following five vectors acting at one point: **A** 2 N, 20°; **B** 3 N, 40°; **C** 4 N, 50°; **D** 5 N, 60°; **E** 8 N, 80°?

[The same notation for the angles is used as for the table above.]

## Components of vectors

If you pulled a barge along a canal, the ideal position would be straight in front of it. However, this would be a problem – you would be in the water! If you walked along the bank, the rope would be at an angle *A* to the canal *(figure 1.16)*. The smaller this angle *A* the better – having a large angle would simply pull the barge into the bank.

It is often necessary to find the components of a vector, usually in two perpendicular directions. This process is called the **resolution of a vector**. What you are really doing is finding the *effectiveness* of the vector along a specified direction. The **component** of a vector along any direction is the magnitude of the vector multiplied by the cosine of the angle between the vector and that direction, so the component of the vector *F* shown in *figure 1.17* is *F* cos (*A*).

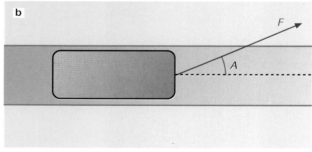

● **Figure 1.16** The most effective way to pull the barge is to keep the angle *A* as small as possible.

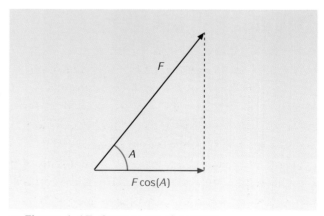

● **Figure 1.17** Component of a vector.

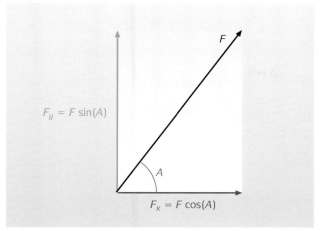

● *Figure 1.18* Components of a vector in two perpendicular directions.

● *Figure 1.19* This person is not lifting the bag in the correct way to avoid back damage.

Imagine pulling the barge along the canal by a rope inclined at an angle to the canal *(figure 1.16)*; the smaller the angle, the more effective the force in the rope (the cosine of the angle gets bigger when the angle gets smaller).

*Figure 1.18* shows the components for a vector in two perpendicular directions (sin *(A)* is the notation for the sine of angle *A*):

component $F_x = F \cos (A)$
component $F_y = F \cos (90 - A) = F \sin (A)$

Resolution of vectors is especially useful when considering problems like the motion of a projectile. Its velocity at any point on its path is the combination of a horizontal component ($v_x$) (constant if there is no air resistance) and a vertical component ($v_y$) which varies as time goes by (because of the action of gravity).

## Bending over and damage to your back

You probably know that the correct way to lift something is by bending your knees and keeping your back straight *(figure 1.19)*. The following calculation (not even involving lifting anything!) shows very clearly why this is. This can be demonstrated very well by using a mop *(figure 1.20)*.

Consider a person bending over so that their spine makes an angle of $\theta°$ with the vertical *(figure 1.21a)*. Their back muscles make an angle of 10° with the spine and have a tension *T*. We will

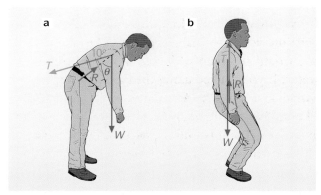

● *Figure 1.20* The tension in the string represents the large tension in the back muscles.

● *Figure 1.21* Forces on a back: **a** straight legs, bent at waist; **b** bent legs, straight back.

assume that the reaction (*R*) at the pelvis acts along the spine. It has been calculated that the weight of the upper body (*W*) is about two-thirds of the total body weight. Resolving at right-angles to the spine we have:

$$W \sin (\theta) = T \sin (10°)$$

For example, if a person with a mass of 50 kg bends over at 60°, then :

$$W = (2/3) \times (50\,\text{kg}) \times g$$
$$= (2/3) \times (50\,\text{kg}) \times (9.8\,\text{m s}^{-2})$$
$$= (2/3) \times 50 \times 9.8\,\text{N}$$

So using the above equation

$$T = \frac{W \sin (\theta)}{\sin (10°)}$$
$$= \frac{(2/3) \times 50 \times 9.8 \times \sin (60°)}{\sin (10°)}$$
$$= 1630\,\text{N}$$

or about 3.3 times body weight.

If the person stands as in *figure 1.21b*, then the tension and reaction are all in the same vertical plane and the tension is reduced.

### SAQ 1.10

What are the $x$ and $y$ components of the vectors shown in *figure 1.22*?

### SAQ 1.11

A horse pulls a barge along a canal using a rope 10 m long. If the barge is 2 m from the bank, the rope is taut and the tension in it is 500 N, what are the components of this force:

**a**  at right-angles to the canal;

**b**  along the line of the canal?

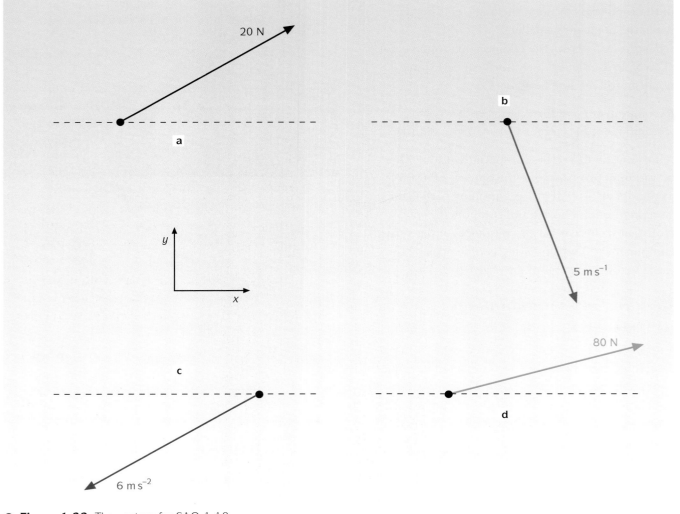

● *Figure 1.22*  The vectors for SAQ 1.10.

# SUMMARY

- All quantities in physics consist of a numerical magnitude and a unit. All units can be expressed in terms of the SI base units.

- If you expand the units for each term of an equation in terms of the base units, you can check whether an equation is balanced (homogeneous).

- It is important to follow sensible scientific guidelines when drawing up tables of results and when plotting graphs.

- Physicists often have to estimate quantities; it is important to ensure that the estimate is of the right order of magnitude.

- When dealing with quantities of atoms and molecules, it is conventional to measure mass and number relative to the carbon-12 atom.

- The relative molecular mass of a substance is the mass of a molecule of the substance divided by 1/12 the mass of a carbon-12 atom.

- The mole is the amount of substance containing the same number of atoms or molecules as the number of atoms in 0.012 kg of carbon-12. This number of atoms is called the Avogadro constant, $L = 6.02 \times 10^{23} \text{mol}^{-1}$.

- Vectors are quantities that must have a direction associated with them. Vectors can be added if direction is taken into account. Vectors can be resolved into components.

# Questions

1 a You are asked to redefine the unit of mass in terms of a quantity which is truly universal. What would you choose and why?

b A distant galaxy can be considered to be a flat disc with a thickness of 5 000 light-years and a radius of 50 000 light-years with one star every cubic light-year (a very rough approximation).
Estimate:
   (i) the number of stars in the galaxy;
   (ii) the number of atoms in 10 g of copper;
   (iii) the number of grains of sand in a bucket of volume 1 dm³ (assume that each grain has a volume of $10^{-3}$ mm³ and ignore the air spaces).

2 a Displacement is the vector measurement of distance. A certain grandfather clock keeps perfect time and has a minute hand that is 20 cm long.
   (i) What is the vector displacement of the tip of the hand from quarter past the hour to half past the hour?
   (ii) What distance has the tip moved in this time?
   (iii) Draw vector diagrams to scale to show the vertical and horizontal components of the velocity of the tip of the hand at quarter past, twenty past, twenty-five past and half past the hour.

b A girl walks along the path with velocity of 1.5 m s$^{-1}$ and as she does so she twirls a conker in a vertical circle on a string 0.8 m long once every second.
What is the velocity of the conker when it is:
   (i) at the top of the circle;
   (ii) half-way down and going downwards?

# Kinematics

● **Figure 2.1** A diving gannet has a high velocity downwards when it enters the water. Clearly the direction of this velocity is important – the bird does not need a high horizontal velocity when it makes its dive.

## Velocity

Velocity is a term you may be familiar with. **Velocity** is the rate of change of displacement. This can be stated as the change in displacement per unit time. This gives the average value of the velocity in equation form as

$$\text{average velocity} = \frac{\text{displacement}}{\text{time}}$$

*Displacement* is used here in preference to *distance* in order to emphasise the directional nature of velocity *(figure 2.1)*. Velocity can be positive or negative, and can be in any stated direction. The other point to realise about velocity is that it is a rate of change: velocity is the gradient of a displacement–time graph. The unit of velocity is the metre per second ($\text{m s}^{-1}$).

This can be made clearer with an example. To say that a driver of a car on a motorway in France is exceeding the speed limit by travelling at 180 kilometres per hour ($\text{km h}^{-1}$) does not mean that the car travels 180 km in one hour. It *does* mean that the rate of travel is equivalent to 180 km in one hour, that is at a rate of 180 000 metres in an hour or 3000 metres in a minute. In other words, the rate of change of displacement is 3000 metres per minute, which is 50 metres per second, $50\,\text{m s}^{-1}$.

When it is not necessary to consider the direction of travel but the rate of change of distance is being found, then the term **speed** is used *(figure 2.2)*. Average speed is given by the equation

$$\text{average speed} = \frac{\text{distance travelled}}{\text{time taken}}$$

Velocity is a vector quantity, as it has direction; speed is a scalar quantity, as it does not have direction.

● **Figure 2.2** A speedometer in a car measures only speed, not velocity.

# Acceleration

Acceleration also is a term you have probably met before *(figure 2.3)*. It too is a rate of change. **Acceleration** is the rate of change of velocity. This can be stated as the change in velocity per unit time, which gives the average value of the acceleration in equation form as

$$\text{average acceleration} = \frac{\text{change in velocity}}{\text{time}}$$

The unit of acceleration can be found from this equation as the unit of velocity divided by the unit of time, i.e. $(\text{m s}^{-1})/\text{s} = \text{m s}^{-2}$. Acceleration is a vector quantity.

The fact that the definitions of velocity and acceleration are similar to one another leads some people to regard them as almost the same as each other. This is not the case. Acceleration is a measure of how rapidly the velocity of some object is changing. It is possible to have an object travelling with high velocity but to have no acceleration at all. It is similarly possible for an object to be stationary and yet to be accelerating. Were this not the case, it would be impossible to move from a stationary position. Other cases that need careful thought are those in which a body has velocity in one direction but acceleration in the opposite direction.

● **Figure 2.3** A large part of the fun of a rollercoaster ride is due to rapid changes of acceleration.

Some of these situations can be illustrated by considering the movement of the ball shown in *figure 2.4*. Air resistance is neglected. The ball is being pulled downwards by the force of gravity all the time, and an object falling near the Earth has a constant acceleration of $9.8 \text{ m s}^{-2}$ if air resistance is negligible (the symbol used for the acceleration of free fall is *g*). This means that the vertical velocity of the ball is changing by 9.8 metres per second each second. While the ball is rising, its upward velocity is decreasing by $9.8 \text{ m s}^{-1}$ each second. If upwards is taken as the positive direction, this is regarded as an acceleration of $-9.8 \text{ m s}^{-2}$, i.e. negative representing downwards. This is a situation in which the velocity is upwards but the acceleration is downwards. After the ball has reached the top of its motion it still has an acceleration downwards of $9.8 \text{ m s}^{-2}$. This too is written $-9.8 \text{ m s}^{-2}$, to show again that it is a downwards acceleration. In other words the acceleration for the whole journey has the constant value of $-9.8 \text{ m s}^{-2}$. This will apply even at the top when, for an instant, the ball is neither rising nor falling, because even at that moment the velocity of the ball is still changing at the same rate. Graphs showing how the displacement, the velocity and the acceleration change with time are shown in *figure 2.4*. Note how the acceleration, shown in red, has a constant value of $-9.8 \text{ m s}^{-2}$; the velocity–time graph, shown in blue, is a straight line with a negative gradient; and the displacement–time graph, shown in black, reaches its maximum value when the velocity is zero.

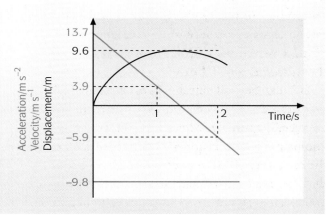

● **Figure 2.4** Graphs of acceleration, velocity and displacement against time for a ball projected horizontally.

● *Figure 2.5* A cricket ball in flight behaves in a similar way to that shown in *figure 2.4*.

## SAQ 2.1

In a 200 m race, run on a straight track, the displacement of an athlete after each second was found from analysis of a video film *(figure 2.6)*. From the values of displacement, the average velocity of the athlete during each second was calculated. This information is displayed in *table 2.1*. Use the data to plot a velocity–time graph for the athlete during this race, and answer the following questions.

**a** How were the values of velocity calculated?

**b** What was the maximum velocity of the athlete?

**c** Calculate the acceleration of the athlete at the 2nd second and at the 9th second.

**d** Why does the graph not quite go through the origin?

**e** Sketch a graph of the athlete's acceleration against time.

**f** What is represented by the total area under the velocity–time graph? Explain your answer.

## Graphical methods

The question about the 200 m race asked you to draw a velocity–time graph for the race. This graph provides a visual display of the data given in the table and shows clearly how the athlete reaches a maximum velocity after 9 s and then slows down for most of the rest of the race. A graph could also have been plotted of displacement against time. Certain features of these graphs should be noted.

Since velocity is the rate of change of displacement, the gradient of a displacement–time graph gives the magnitude of the velocity.

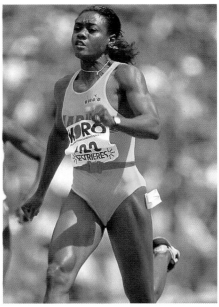

● *Figure 2.6* Merlene Ottey competing in a 200 m race. The time taken to complete the race is usually the only physical quantity measured; but how does the velocity change during the race?

| Time /s | Displacement /m | Average velocity during each second /m s$^{-1}$ |
|---|---|---|
| 0 | 0 | |
| 1 | 3.0 | 3.0 |
| 2 | 10.1 | 7.1 |
| 3 | 18.3 | 8.2 |
| 4 | 27.4 | 9.1 |
| 5 | 36.9 | 9.5 |
| 6 | 46.7 | 9.8 |
| 7 | 56.7 | 10.0 |
| 8 | 66.8 | 10.1 |
| 9 | 77.0 | 10.2 |
| 10 | 87.0 | 10.0 |
| 11 | 97.0 | 10.0 |
| 12 | 106.9 | 9.9 |
| 13 | 116.8 | 9.9 |
| 14 | 126.8 | 10.0 |
| 15 | 136.6 | 9.8 |
| 16 | 146.4 | 9.8 |
| 17 | 156.1 | 9.7 |
| 18 | 165.8 | 9.7 |
| 19 | 175.4 | 9.6 |
| 20 | 185.0 | 9.6 |
| 21 | 194.5 | 9.5 |
| 21.64 | 200.0 | |

● *Table 2.1* Data for SAQ 2.1

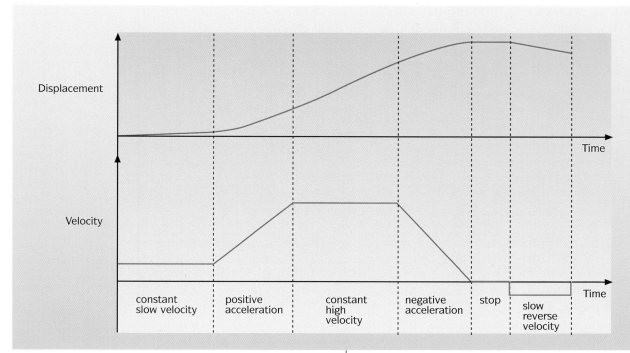

● *Figure 2.7* Velocity–time and displacement–time graphs for the same journey. The gradient (slope) of a displacement–time graph gives the velocity.

Similarly, since acceleration is the rate of change of velocity, the gradient of a velocity–time graph gives the magnitude of the acceleration. These two graphs, *for the same journey*, are shown in *figure 2.7*.

A velocity–time graph is particularly useful since it is possible to show that the area beneath a velocity–time graph gives the distance. If you plot a velocity–time graph for something moving

with a non-zero constant velocity, the graph is a horizontal line. The velocity multiplied by the time, which gives the displacement, also gives the area of a rectangle on the graph, and this rectangle is the area beneath the graph. This can be extended to motion in which the velocity is not constant, as is done in the following section.

# Equations of motion for uniform acceleration

*Figure 2.8* enables the displacement *s* to be calculated when an object has a constant acceleration from velocity *u* to velocity *v* in time *t*. In this work *u* is the symbol always used for the velocity at the start of any particular acceleration and *v* is used for the velocity at the finish of the acceleration. The acceleration is given by

$$\text{acceleration} = \frac{\text{change in velocity}}{\text{time}}$$

$$a = \frac{v - u}{t} \qquad (2.1)$$

giving

$$v - u = at$$

as shown on the graph.

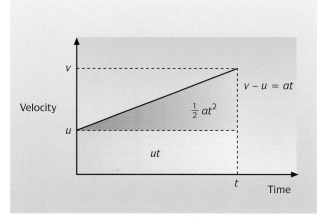

● *Figure 2.8* The gradient of a velocity–time graph gives the acceleration, $a = (v - u)/t$. The area underneath a velocity–time graph gives the displacement, $s = ut + \frac{1}{2}at^2$.

The displacement is the area beneath the graph, the shaded area, and can be calculated in different ways. The obvious way, from the graph, is the area of the bottom rectangle, $ut$, plus the area of the triangle $\frac{1}{2}at^2$. The displacement can also be found by subtracting the area of the triangle from the area of the large rectangle, $vt$, or by finding the average height of the area, $\frac{1}{2}(v + u)$, and multiplying this by the time. These three approaches give rise to the following three equations.

$$s = ut + \tfrac{1}{2}at^2 \qquad (2.2)$$
$$s = vt - \tfrac{1}{2}at^2 \qquad (2.3)$$
$$s = \frac{v + u}{2}\, t \qquad (2.4)$$

Algebraically eliminating $t$ from any pair of these equations gives the further equation

$$v^2 = u^2 + 2as \qquad (2.5)$$

The equations above are called **equations of motion**. They *only* apply for acceleration that is constant. Do not apply them just because you happen to know, say, a velocity, a time and an acceleration. You must also know that the acceleration is constant. The following questions can be answered using these equations. The first thing you will need to do is to decide which equation is appropriate. Use the equation that contains the three quantities you know and the one you are trying to find.

● *Figure 2.9* Designing motorways is a complicated business. Even the length and slope of a slip road have to be worked out carefully (see SAQ 2.2).

## SAQ 2.2

A motorway designer can assume that cars approaching a motorway enter a slip road with a velocity of $10\,\mathrm{m\,s^{-1}}$ and need to reach a velocity of $30\,\mathrm{m\,s^{-1}}$ before joining the motorway *(figure 2.9)*. If an acceleration of $4.0\,\mathrm{m\,s^{-2}}$ is assumed, how long should the slip road be?

## SAQ 2.3

A train is travelling at $50\,\mathrm{m\,s^{-1}}$ when the driver applies the brakes and gives the train a constant acceleration of $-0.5\,\mathrm{m\,s^{-2}}$ for $100\,\mathrm{s}$. Describe what happens to the train and find how far it travels during the $100\,\mathrm{s}$.

## SAQ 2.4

The graph in *figure 2.10* shows the speed of two cars A and B, which are travelling in the same direction over a period of time of $40\,\mathrm{s}$. Car A, travelling at a constant speed of $40\,\mathrm{m\,s^{-1}}$, overtakes car B at time $t = 0$. In order to catch up with car A, car B immediately accelerates uniformly for $20\,\mathrm{s}$ to reach a constant speed of $50\,\mathrm{m\,s^{-1}}$. Calculate:

**a** how far A travels during the first $20\,\mathrm{s}$,

**b** the acceleration and distance of travel of B during the first $20\,\mathrm{s}$,

**c** the additional time taken for B to catch up with A,

**d** how far each car will have then travelled since $t = 0$,

**e** the maximum distance between the cars before B catches up with A.

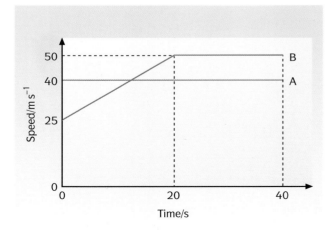

● *Figure 2.10* Speed–time graphs for two cars, A and B (see SAQ 2.4).

# Falling objects

So far in this chapter it has been assumed that when an object falls it moves vertically with a constant downwards acceleration of $9.8\,\mathrm{m\,s^{-2}}$. In the absence of air resistance, the constant downwards acceleration is true, but the object may not be moving vertically. Clearly a football in free fall does not usually only move vertically. This is because it is started by being kicked forwards; it has a horizontal velocity as well as a vertical velocity. It is possible to regard these two components of velocity completely independently, as is done in the following example.

In a toy, a ball-bearing is lifted through a height of $0.40\,\mathrm{m}$ and then projected horizontally from a ledge with a velocity of $2.4\,\mathrm{m\,s^{-1}}$, as shown in *figure 2.11*. Find how long it takes to reach the floor and at what horizontal distance from its starting point it will hit the floor. Show on a sketch graph the path of the ball-bearing's flight.

Information available is: vertical distance of fall, $0.40\,\mathrm{m}$; acceleration, $9.8\,\mathrm{m\,s^{-2}}$ downwards; starting velocity downwards, $0\,\mathrm{m\,s^{-1}}$; starting velocity horizontally, $2.4\,\mathrm{m\,s^{-1}}$.

Use equation $s = ut + \frac{1}{2}at^2$ (where $t$ is the time of fall) to get

$$0.40 = 0 + \tfrac{1}{2} \times 9.8 \times t^2$$
$$0.80/9.8 = t^2$$
$$t = 0.29\,\mathrm{s}$$

During this time the ball-bearing has had a constant horizontal velocity of $2.4\,\mathrm{m\,s^{-1}}$, so will have travelled $0.286 \times 2.4$ metres horizontally. Its horizontal distance from the starting point is therefore $0.69\,\mathrm{m}$.

To find the ball-bearing's position at intermediate times, it is convenient to use a table *(table 2.2)*. The downward distance is found by repeated use of the equation $s = ut + \frac{1}{2}at^2$. The path is shown in *figure 2.11* together with arrows representing horizontal and vertical velocities throughout the flight. While the vertical velocity increases due to the downward acceleration, the horizontal velocity remains constant.

# Terminal velocity

When an object is dropped, air resistance is often neglected. In fact, even for a diver making a $10\,\mathrm{m}$ high-board dive, the error involved in making this simplification is very small. On the other hand, clearly, the same simplification cannot be made for a parachutist, since parachutists rely on air resistance to limit the maximum velocity of descent to that which does not cause injury when they hit the ground *(figures 2.12 and 2.13)*. Whether or not air resistance needs to be taken into account cannot be answered simply. The science of movement of objects through the air is called ballistics. It is an old and complex science, which has had military importance for such objects as cannonballs, shells and bombs.

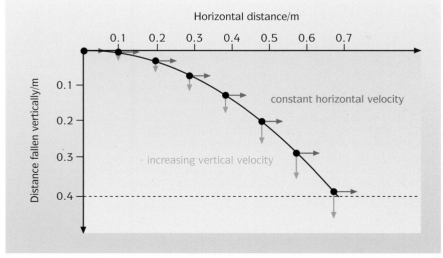

● *Figure 2.11* This shows the movement of, and the forces on, a ball projected horizontally from a ledge (see the example of the toy).

| Time/s | Downward distance/m | Horizontal distance/m |
|---|---|---|
| 0 | 0 | 0 |
| 0.04 | 0.008 | 0.096 |
| 0.08 | 0.032 | 0.192 |
| 0.12 | 0.071 | 0.288 |
| 0.16 | 0.125 | 0.384 |
| 0.20 | 0.196 | 0.480 |
| 0.24 | 0.282 | 0.576 |
| 0.28 | 0.384 | 0.672 |

● *Table 2.2* Data for the toy example

● **Figure 2.12** A parachutist in free-fall – low air resistance.

● **Figure 2.13** A parachutist with the canopy unfolded – high air resistance.

Here a qualitative description only is given, and that for the simpler situation of vertical fall. The force that the air exerts on an object moving through it, called the **air resistance**, always acts in a direction opposite to the object's velocity. The magnitude of the air resistance depends on the density of the air and on the speed of the object through the air. Concorde aircraft (*figure 2.14*) cruise at very high altitude because the density of the air decreases with altitude

● **Figure 2.14**

and therefore air resistance is reduced – an important factor when travelling in excess of the speed of sound. *Figure 2.15* shows a sequence of positions of an object falling vertically from rest. The weight $W$ of the object is constant throughout. The lengths of the arrows represent the sizes of the forces. At the instant when the object is released, as shown in A, its velocity is zero, there is no air resistance and so it accelerates at $9.8\,\mathrm{m\,s^{-2}}$. By the time it reaches position B, it has a downward velocity and so, as a result of moving through the air, has a force of air resistance acting on it. This force acts upwards, so reducing the resultant force on the object and hence reducing its acceleration. As the object's velocity increases, the air resistance also increases. This means that the resultant force and the corresponding acceleration become less and less (C and D). Eventually, as shown in E, the force of air resistance becomes equal in magnitude to the weight, the resultant force is then zero and so the object ceases to accelerate. This maximum velocity of fall is called the **terminal velocity**.

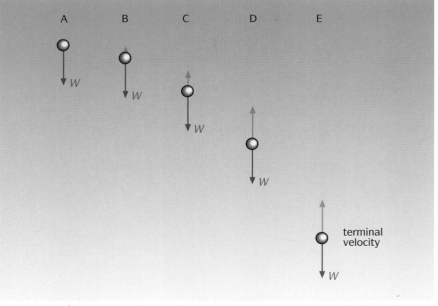

● **Figure 2.15** The forces of gravity and air resistance on a falling object at regular time intervals. Its vertical position is also indicated.

● *Figure 2.16* Top-class tennis players can make a ball travel very fast indeed. But what would Wimbledon be like if the matches were held on the Moon (see SAQ 2.5)?

### SAQ 2.5

A tennis player hits a tennis ball horizontally with a velocity of $56\,\mathrm{m\,s^{-1}}$ when it is at a height of $2.5\,\mathrm{m}$ above the ground *(figure 2.16)*. Ignoring air resistance, find the horizontal distance the ball will travel before hitting the ground. If it were conceivable to play the same tennis stroke, with the same velocity of ball, on a flat surface on the Moon, how far horizontally would the ball then go without hitting the ground? [The acceleration due to gravity on the Moon is $1.6\,\mathrm{m\,s^{-2}}$.]

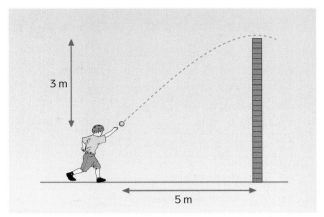

● *Figure 2.17*

### SAQ 2.6

A boy is trying to throw a ball over a wall. He is standing $5\,\mathrm{m}$ away from a wall, whose top is $3.0\,\mathrm{m}$ higher than his hand at the instant he releases the ball *(figure 2.17)*. Show that, if the ball is thrown with a velocity of $11.1\,\mathrm{m\,s^{-1}}$ at an angle of $45°$ to the horizontal, the ball will just get over the wall.

### SAQ 2.7

The force of air resistance ($F$) acting on a parachute is given by the equation

$$F = 83 + 14.6v^2$$

where $v$ is the velocity in $\mathrm{m\,s^{-1}}$ and $F$ is measured in newtons (N). A parachutist of total weight $680\,\mathrm{N}$ is descending. Calculate the terminal velocity of the parachutist.

# SUMMARY

■ Average velocity = $\dfrac{\text{displacement}}{\text{time}}$

■ Acceleration = $\dfrac{\text{change in velocity}}{\text{time}}$.

■ Equations of motion:

$$v - u = at$$
$$s = ut + \tfrac{1}{2}at^2$$
$$s = vt - \tfrac{1}{2}at^2$$
$$s = \frac{v + u}{2}\,t$$
$$v^2 = u^2 + 2as.$$

■ The gradient of a displacement–time graph gives the magnitude of the velocity.

■ The gradient of a velocity–time graph gives the magnitude of the acceleration.

■ The area beneath a velocity–time graph gives the distance travelled.

■ For projectiles, the horizontal and vertical components of velocity can be treated independently. In the absence of air resistance, the horizontal component of velocity is constant while the vertical component of velocity downwards increases at a rate of $9.8\,\mathrm{m\,s^{-2}}$.

■ An object falling freely in air accelerates until a terminal velocity is reached. At this velocity there is no acceleration because the force of air resistance, upwards, on the object is equal and opposite to the weight of the object.

## Questions

1 In a motorway crash, a car travelling (illegally) at $50 \, \text{m s}^{-1}$ stops in a distance of 4.0 m. Calculate the acceleration of the car and the time it takes to stop.

   Seat belts would probably break during such a crash. Suggest why seat belts are not made stronger.

2 Draw a sketch graph to show how the velocity of a ball-bearing changes when it is dropped from rest to fall freely in air. Draw a second velocity–time graph to show what happens when the experiment is repeated with a table tennis ball of the same mass.

   Explain why it is possible for a small animal to fall from a considerable height without any injury being caused when it reaches the ground.

## Chapter three

# Dynamics

**By the end of this chapter you should be able to:**

1 use the term *mass* correctly;

2 define and use the terms *momentum* and *force*;

3 state and use Newton's laws of motion;

4 state and use the principle of conservation of momentum.

## Mass

At the Bureau International des Poids et Mesures, Sèvres, near Paris, there is a cylindrical block of a platinum–iridium alloy. This block of metal has a mass of *exactly* one kilogram. The word 'exactly' is important. It is not often that any physical quantity is known exactly, because any measuring instrument must produce some uncertainty about the quantity it is measuring. Here, however, the block in question is exactly one kilogram because, by international agreement, everyone accepts the block as being the standard of mass. It is *the* kilogram. All other masses are measured by instruments that have, effectively, been calibrated against the Sèvres kilogram. Because it is so important for scientists and engineers to be able to compare their measurements with one another, it is essential that standards are established. In this case the kilogram as the standard of mass is kept in specially controlled conditions. It is made out of the platinum–iridium alloy so that its surface will not oxidise, as this would increase its mass, and it must not be touched by hand as this would add grease to its surface. The mass of this block is kept constant as far as is humanly possible. It would not matter if it was taken to any other place on Earth, or up in a satellite, or to the Moon. Its mass would be one kilogram anywhere. This constant nature of mass is one of the key facts in distinguishing between weight and mass. *Weight* is a force, which varies from place to place. On the Moon, for example, the weight of an object is different from its weight

on the Earth; its *mass* though does not change (*figure 3.1*). The mass of an object is constant because wherever it is, it always requires the same total force on it for a given acceleration. A term sometimes used instead of mass is *inertia*. This is perhaps a better word than mass since it implies more clearly that it is a measure of the property of the body that resists change in motion. The **mass** (inertia) of any object is a measure of the reluctance of the object to accelerate.

## Momentum

The **momentum** of an object is defined by the equation

$$\text{momentum} = \text{mass} \times \text{velocity}$$

Momentum (plural momenta) is a vector quantity with direction always the same as the direction of the velocity. It has the unit $\mathrm{kg\,m\,s^{-1}}$. (This will be shown to be the same unit as the newton second (N s).) Momentum is a useful quantity to use, particularly in problems involving collisions. Reasons for this will be given later. At this stage it is simply necessary to understand how to calculate the momentum, as shown in *table 3.1*.

● *Figure 3.1* A man walking on the Moon has the same mass as he has on the Earth, but his weight is less because the force of gravity is smaller.

| Object | Mass/kg | Velocity/m s⁻¹ | Momentum/N s |
|---|---|---|---|
| Hockey ball | 0.16 | 25 | 4.0 |
| Car | 1000 | 25 | 25 000 |
| Electron in TV tube | $9.1 \times 10^{-31}$ | $1.0 \times 10^7$ | $9.1 \times 10^{-24}$ |
| Moon | $7.4 \times 10^{22}$ | 1000 | $7.4 \times 10^{25}$ |

● **Table 3.1** Momenta of some objects

## SAQ 3.1

What is the momentum of a sprinter of mass 50 kg when at the end of an indoor 60 m race and travelling with a velocity of 9.4 m s⁻¹?

## SAQ 3.2

What is the change in the momentum of a snooker ball, of mass 0.350 kg, if it moves so that it hits at right-angles on to the edge of the snooker table at 2.8 m s⁻¹ and leaves the edge, also at right-angles to it, at 2.5 m s⁻¹? (The answer to this question is *not* 0.105 N s.)

# Newton's laws

## *Newton's first law*

Until the time of Newton, the relationship between motion and force was vague. It was simply a question of 'if you push it, it moves; if you push harder, it moves faster'. Newton realised the importance of acceleration rather than velocity. He was the first person formally to state that an object with zero total force acting on it will continue to move with constant velocity. He was forced to this conclusion by considering the motion of bodies that he observed in space. These move continuously and nothing is required to keep them moving.

In the laboratory, a linear air track can be used to demonstrate the ability of a moving object to coast along, as shown in *figure 3.2*. The air track must be set horizontally. Then a mass on the air track supported by its cushion of air has zero total force acting on it. If it is at rest, it will remain at rest; if it is moving, it continues to move with constant velocity. This is true for all objects.

The following statement is known as Newton's **first law of motion**: If no resultant force acts on it, a body at rest will remain at rest, and a body moving with constant velocity continues to move with the same constant velocity.

This law makes a good definition of *force*, a vector quantity. A **force** is that which can change the state of rest of an object, or its state of uniform motion in a straight line.

### Experiment to find acceleration of a glider on an air track

Set up the air track either, and preferably, so that the times at which the glider passes various photocells can be measured and recorded, or so that a ticker-tape and ticker-timer can be used to measure the glider's speed as shown in *figure 3.2*. Apply a constant force to the glider for a known distance. It is easy to do this by hanging a weight attached to the glider by a thread passing over a pulley. When the weight hits the floor, the force applied to the glider suddenly falls to zero. When everything is set up, start the experiment by releasing the glider. Use the recorded times to calculate the velocity of the glider at known times from the start and plot a graph of velocity against time. Calculate the acceleration during the two sections of the graph.

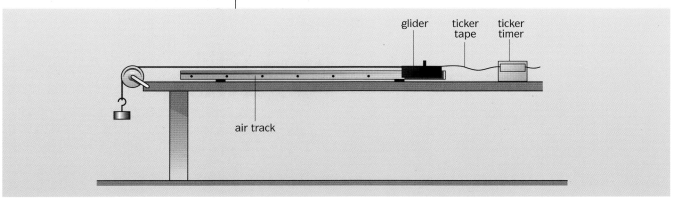

● **Figure 3.2**

## Newton's second law

The experimental investigation described above illustrates that zero force produces zero acceleration. It also shows that, when a constant resultant force is applied to an object, a constant acceleration is produced. The investigation could have been extended to show that the magnitude of the acceleration produced by a force is inversely proportional to the mass of the accelerating object. Newton expressed this in his **second law of motion** by stating that: the rate of change of momentum of an object is proportional to the total force applied to it.

## Newton's first and second laws in equation form

The second law can be written as

force ∝ rate of change of momentum

$$\text{force} = \text{constant} \times \frac{\text{momentum change}}{\text{time}}$$

$$= k\,\frac{mv - mu}{t} \qquad \text{assuming constant mass}$$

$$= km\,\frac{v - u}{t}$$

$$= kma$$

The unit of force, the newton (N), is defined as the force necessary to give a mass of 1 kg an acceleration of $1\,\mathrm{m\,s^{-2}}$.

The effect of defining the newton in this way is to make the constant, $k$, in the above equation equal to 1. This gives the important equation

force/N = (mass/kg) × (acceleration/m s$^{-2}$)

This equation summarises Newton's first and second laws.

## Newton's third law

This law is one of the foundation stones of science. It can be applied to interactions on an astronomical or atomic scale as well as to everyday phenomena. It demonstrates the genius of Newton, but, as with many fundamental principles, its importance is difficult to appreciate at first. The law itself deals with the forces of interaction between any two objects. The objects might both be massive objects like the Earth and the Sun, but one could be massive and one could be tiny, the Earth and you, for example.

In a modern form Newton's **third law of motion** states: If object A exerts a force on object B, then object B exerts an equal and opposite force on object A; both forces are of the same type.

If one of these forces is a gravitational force, then both of them are gravitational forces. Note that there is no reference to the objects having to be at rest: the law *always* applies. If you hold the rope in a tug of war, which is stationary, the force you exert on the rope is the same in magnitude and the opposite in direction at all instants as the force that the rope exerts on you. The law still applies if you win or if you lose the tug of war. You then exert a smaller or a larger force on the rope; it exerts a smaller or a larger force on you.

Consider the collision between a train and a fly. The third law states that the force that the fly exerts on the train is equal and opposite to the force that the train exerts on the fly. At first sight this seems nonsensical, but consider further the effects of these two equal and opposite forces. The train has a force of, say, 0.5 N acting on it in a backward direction. This is a tiny force as far as the train is concerned and so it makes no apparent difference to the motion of the train. The fly has a forward force of 0.5 N acting on it. This is a huge force as far as the fly is concerned – enough to give it a huge forwards acceleration as it is squashed flat against the windscreen of the train.

The key to understanding Newton's third law lies in realising that the two forces are acting on different objects. Clear force diagrams are essential before any calculations of acceleration are done. You need to consider one object at a time and to draw all the forces on that object only. Do not be tempted to draw forces on a single diagram for several objects. This makes it very difficult, if not impossible, to show the two forces referred to in Newton's third law. A diagram that shows just one object and the forces on it, is called a **free-body diagram**. On a free-body diagram of an object only one of the two forces referred to in Newton's third law can appear. The second force acts on a *different* object and must therefore appear on a different free-body diagram. When drawing free-body diagrams there should be a force acting on the body at every point at which it touches something else. Its weight must also be shown.

*Figure 3.3* is a photograph of a car towing a caravan; *figures 3.4a* and *3.4b* show free-body diagrams of the car, which is driven by its rear wheels, and the caravan. The force the car exerts on the caravan is shown on the free-body diagram of the caravan; the force the caravan exerts on the car is always *exactly* equal and opposite to this and is shown on the free-body diagram of the car. If the values of the forces are known, then these two diagrams can be used to find the acceleration of the car and of the caravan. (Why must these be the same?) Where are the equal and opposite forces to all the other forces shown acting on the car and the caravan?

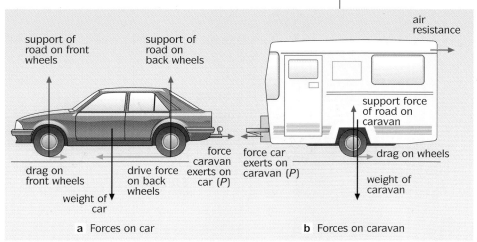

● **Figure 3.3** There are many more forces acting on this car and caravan than you might think *(see figure 3.4)*.

# Friction

When free-body force diagrams are drawn, contact forces between one object and another must be included. The direction in which these forces act can be difficult to find. Consider a book at rest on a sloping surface. The book is in contact with the surface, although in *figure 3.5* it is shown slightly separated from the surface so that the forces on the book can be drawn clearly. The pull of gravity on the book, its weight $W$, must be drawn in. Since the book is not accelerating, the resultant force on the book is zero, and so the surface must exert a contact force, $C$, on the book that is equal and opposite to the weight. This contact force is often resolved into two components as shown. The first component is a force at right-angles to the surface, and is labelled the normal force, $N$; the second component is a force acting parallel to the surface, and is the force of friction, $F$. In this context the word 'normal' means 'at right-angles to'.

The force of friction is very important because it enables many everyday activities to be carried out. Without friction, walking, eating, knitting, sitting, moving, driving, climbing and most other activities would be impossible *(figures 3.6 and 3.7)*. Because friction is so familiar a force, it often gets overlooked. Certain features of the frictional force need to be clearly established. First, and obviously, its magnitude depends on the nature of the

a Forces on car      b Forces on caravan

● **Figure 3.4** Free-body diagrams of a car towing a caravan. Such diagrams are drawn to show the forces acting on objects, as clearly as possible.

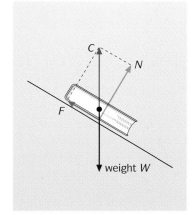

● **Figure 3.5** Free-body diagram of a book at rest on a slope. There must be a force of friction acting on the book up the slope to keep it at rest.

● *Figure 3.6* A rock-climber, such as Isabelle Patissier, depends on friction between the toes of her boots and the rock surface.

● *Figure 3.7* Ice or snow is much smoother than a road surface, so there is much less friction exerted by the ice or snow on a tyre when a vehicle brakes.

surfaces (how slippery they are). Secondly, its magnitude also depends on the value of the normal force – if you push hard on something you may say that you 'get a better grip'. Thirdly, it does not necessarily have a constant value. The force of friction can have any value between a maximum value forwards and (usually) the same maximum value backwards. Learning to walk, for a baby, is experimenting, by trial and error, to adjust the frictional force between her feet and the ground to that which is needed either to propel her forward at one instant (friction force forward) or to stop her foot moving forward a moment later (friction force backwards).

If the rear-wheel drive car in *figure 3.8* is being driven along the road, the force of friction at the front wheel is a backward force: it contributes to the total drag on the car, and a car designer will try to make this force as small as possible. The frictional force on the back wheels, however, is in the direction of movement of the car because these wheels are connected to the engine. These are the driving wheels of the car, and the force of friction is

the force that is causing the car to move. If the driver takes her foot off the accelerator pedal and transfers it to the brake pedal, then the rate of rotation of the wheels is reduced by the brakes. As a result, the frictional force at the front wheel is increased and the driving force at the back wheel is changed into a braking force (*figure 3.9*).

## SAQ 3.3

Calculate the force required to give a satellite of mass 600 kg an acceleration of $55\,\mathrm{m\,s^{-2}}$.

## SAQ 3.4

Calculate the acceleration that would be produced if a force of 1200 N acts on a mass of 80 kg. If this mass is being accelerated from rest, how far will it travel before its velocity reaches $45\,\mathrm{m\,s^{-1}}$?

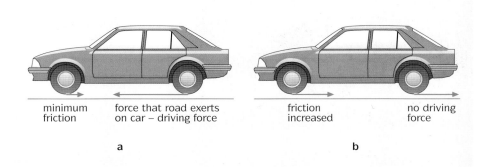

a       minimum friction     force that road exerts on car – driving force

b       friction increased     no driving force

● *Figure 3.8* The forces acting on   **a** a car being driven;   **b** a car braking.

● *Figure 3.9* If a car brakes heavily, a tyre may stop rotating, and the friction between tyre and track heats the rubber and causes it to burn and smoke.

## SAQ 3.5

In an emergency stop, a car of mass 800 kg, driven by a driver of mass 80 kg, needs to stop from a speed of 30 m s$^{-1}$ in a distance of 40 m. What braking force will be required? What will be the effect on this emergency if there are additional passengers in the car with total mass of 200 kg?

## SAQ 3.6

A high-speed lift in a tower block has a mass of 800 kg and can carry passengers up to a total mass of 600 kg. What tension is necessary in the support cable if the lift and its passengers are to reach an upward velocity of 11 m s$^{-1}$ within 5 s of starting? (The answer to this question is not 3080 N.)

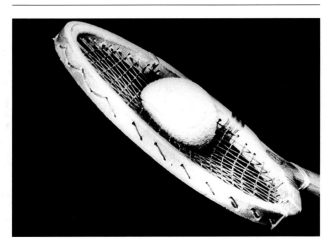

● *Figure 3.10* A tennis ball is squashed when hit by a racquet. This is because the front of the ball is undergoing a large change in momentum, while the back of the ball is still moving with its initial momentum.

# Conservation of momentum

Newton's laws can be applied when there is a collision between two objects. Consider a tennis racquet hitting a tennis ball *(figure 3.10)*. The third law states that the force that the racquet applies to the ball in the forward direction is equal and opposite to the force that the ball exerts on the racquet in the backward direction. These forces are not constant but must be exerted for the same length of time. The two forces may change in the way shown in *figure 3.11* and are equivalent to a constant force of 150 N being applied for 2 milliseconds (2 ms), or a constant force of 100 N being applied for 3 ms. Using Newton's law

$$F = ma$$

or

$$F = m\frac{v - u}{t}$$

So

$$Ft = mv - mu$$

Since $Ft$ has the same value for both the racquet and the ball, this equation implies that the increase in the momentum of the ball, $F \times t$, is 150 N × 2 ms or 0.3 N s, and the decrease in the momentum of the racquet has exactly the same value because the force

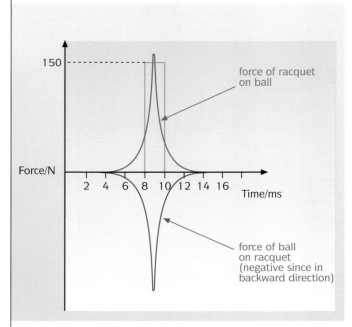

● *Figure 3.11* Changes in forces when a racquet hits a ball.

on it is in the opposite direction. This is true for all collisions. If one of the colliding objects gains momentum, the other must lose an equal amount of momentum. This result is summarised by the **law of conservation of momentum**, which states that the total momentum of an isolated system cannot be changed. An isolated system is any object or collection of objects on which no force is exerted by any external object. If the isolated system considered is the whole Universe, then the law becomes: the total momentum of the Universe is constant.

One interesting consequence of the law of conservation of momentum can be demonstrated in a space capsule. If astronauts push something forward, their bodies move backwards. (There is no friction to stop this.) Astronauts find it very difficult to use tools because of this and need to be strapped down for many jobs *(figure 3.12)*.

In collisions, the forces acting often occur for a brief interval of time, and it is difficult to measure the size of these forces. The example with the tennis ball illustrates that calculations depend upon being able to use the product *Ft*. This is equal to the change in momentum and is measured in the unit newton second (N s). It is called the **impulse** of the force.

Note that the law of conservation of momentum makes no reference to any conditions. The colliding objects may bounce off one another or may stick to one another; they may even explode. Momentum will still be conserved. Therefore, if you have a problem involving a collision, always start by considering momentum. Do not apply the law of conservation of energy, because there may be a loss of kinetic energy: there will never be a loss of momentum. (See chapter 5, page 39, for details about kinetic energy.)

We shall now look at an example. The driver of a car involved in a motorway pile-up claims that he

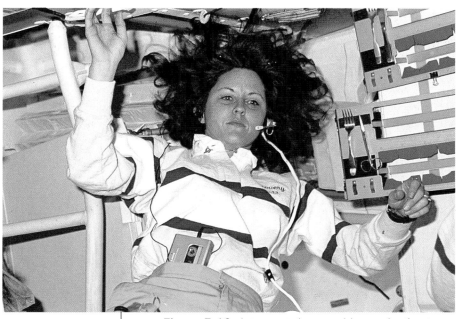

● *Figure 3.12* Astronauts have problems adapting to life in orbit because of the law of conservation of momentum.

had initially stopped 20 m behind the car in front of him and had been hit from his rear by a lorry, which had become embedded in his car. The police investigate his claim that he was not responsible for driving into the car in front of him and have the following additional information:

mass of lorry = 5000 kg
speed of lorry on collision = $18\,\mathrm{m\,s^{-1}}$
mass of car = 1000 kg
frictional force on car and lorry = 36 000 N

Does the physics of the problem support the driver's account of the collision?

Apply the law of conservation of momentum. So

$$\frac{\text{momentum of lorry}}{\text{before collision}} = \frac{\text{momentum of car and}}{\text{lorry after collision}}$$

$$5000\,\mathrm{kg} \times 18\,\mathrm{m\,s^{-1}} = 5000V + 1000V$$

where *V* is speed of car and lorry the instant after the collision. So

$$5000 \times 18 = 6000V$$
$$V = \frac{5000 \times 18}{6000} = 15\,\mathrm{m\,s^{-1}}$$

Also

acceleration of car and lorry together

$$= \frac{\text{force}}{\text{mass}} = \frac{-36\,000\,\text{N}}{6000\,\text{kg}} = -6.0\,\text{m s}^{-2}$$

Since for uniform acceleration $v^2 = u^2 + 2as$ and since the final speed is zero (initial speed $u = V = 15\,\text{m s}^{-1}$)

$$0 = 15^2 + (2 \times -6 \times s)$$
$$225 = 12s$$
$$s = 19\,\text{m (to 2 significant figures)}$$

The driver may be correct. While the calculation shows that it is unlikely that he was pushed as far forward as 20 m, it does show that the lorry behind him could have pushed him forward a considerable distance. In cases of serious injury, forensic scientists and the Road Research Laboratory carry out such calculations and measurements for the courts. The data for the above example have, however, been simplified.

## SAQ 3.7

A space vehicle of mass 4200 kg needs to have its velocity adjusted from 8680 m s$^{-1}$ to 8750 m s$^{-1}$. Assuming that this is carried out in a straight line and with little change to the total mass of the vehicle, find for how long its rocket motors must be switched on if they exert a force of 1200 N on the vehicle in the required direction *(figure 3.13)*.

(It is more direct to answer this question using
$Ft = mv - mu$
rather than
force = mass × acceleration
although the two approaches are equivalent.)

## SAQ 3.8

A golf ball has a mass of 0.046 kg. What average force does a golf club exert on a golf ball during a contact time of 1.3 ms if the ball's velocity immediately after being struck is 50 m s$^{-1}$ *(figure 3.14)*?

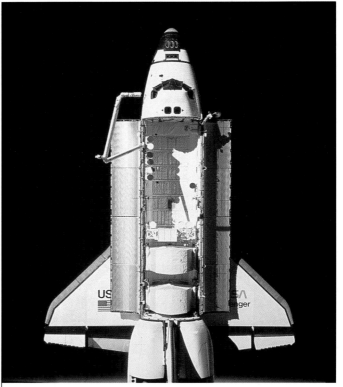

● *Figure 3.13* The Space Shuttle uses several sets of adjuster rockets (see SAQ 3.7).

● *Figure 3.14* A golfer in the process of hitting a ball (see SAQ 3.8). How are conservation of momentum and the concept of impulse involved?

# SUMMARY

■ Mass is a scalar property of an object and does not change as it moves from place to place. Mass is a measure of the reluctance of the object to accelerate. It is measured in kilograms.

■ Momentum is a vector. For an object it is the product of the object's mass and its velocity. It is measured in newton seconds.

■ Newton's first law: If no resultant force acts on it, a body at rest will remain at rest, and a body moving with constant velocity will continue to move with the same constant velocity.

■ Newton's second law: The rate of change of momentum of an object is proportional to the total force applied to it.

■ Newton's third law: If object A exerts a force on object B, then object B exerts an equal and opposite force on object A; both forces are of the same type.

■ Newton's first law gives a definition of force as that which can change the state of rest of an object, or its state of uniform motion in a straight line.

■ The following equation summarises both of Newton's first two laws:

force/N = (mass/kg) × (acceleration/m s$^{-2}$).

■ The law of conservation of momentum states that the total momentum of an isolated system is constant.

# Questions

1 SAQ 2.7 dealt with a parachute on which the force of air resistance ($F$) acting was given by the equation

$$F = 83 + 14.6v^2$$

where $v$ is the velocity in m s$^{-1}$ and $F$ is measured in newtons. If a parachutist of total weight 680 N is descending, calculate the acceleration of the parachutist when she has a downward velocity of 5.0 m s$^{-1}$. Is there a stage in her descent when she might have a downward velocity of 24 m s$^{-1}$? Calculate, for this velocity, the acceleration of the parachutist. In what direction is this acceleration? Explain what this means.

2 An aeroplane with no passengers in it has a mass of 120 000 kg when ready for take-off. Its engines give it a thrust of 600 000 N and it needs to reach a velocity of 60 m s$^{-1}$ in order to take off. What length of runway is required?

If the plane is loaded with 360 passengers and their luggage, the mass of the plane increases by 36 000 kg and the take-off velocity increases to 70 m s$^{-1}$. Calculate the length of runway required for the loaded aeroplane.

Why, in practice are runways considerably longer than this type of calculation predicts?

3 The Earth has a mass of $6.0 \times 10^{24}$ kg and its circular orbit around the Sun has a radius of $1.5 \times 10^{11}$ m.
  a How long does it take for the Earth to travel once around the Sun?
  b Calculate the speed of the Earth in its orbit around the Sun.
  c Show that, if the Earth unfortunately bumped into and absorbed a stationary lump of matter of mass $1.0 \times 10^{18}$ kg, the Earth's speed would be reduced by 0.005 m s$^{-1}$.

# *Forces*

## Equilibrium

If the resultant force on a point object is zero, the object is said to be in **equilibrium**. Note that this does not necessarily mean that the object is stationary: it may be moving in a straight line with constant velocity. The resultant force on the object shown in *figure 4.1a* is zero, because the two 15 N forces are equal and opposite to one another. In *figure 4.1b* the resultant force is also zero because the angles have been arranged so that the sum of the 5 N and the 12 N forces is 15 N to the left, and this balances the 15 N force to the right. If the triangle ABC is inspected, it will be seen that each side represents one of the three forces. This is shown on a separate diagram, *figure 4.1c*, and illustrates a general principle called the **triangle of forces**: If three forces are acting on a point object that is in equilibrium, they can be represented in magnitude and direction by the sides of a triangle taken in order.

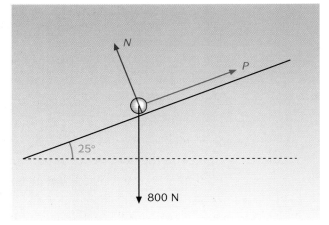

● *Figure 4.2*

### SAQ 4.1

An object of weight 800 N, treated as a point object, is held at rest on a 25° slope by applying a force *P* to it along the slope, as shown in *figure 4.2*. The normal contact force *N* on the object is also shown. Draw a triangle of forces to represent these three forces and find, both by scale drawing and by calculation, the values of *P* and *N*. (Your answers should agree to within 5 N.)

## Centre of gravity

Any object is made up of a large number of individual particles, each of which has its own weight. If all of these particles had to be considered separately, problems concerning the acceleration and stability of objects would become impossibly difficult. The difficulty can be overcome by a mathematical convenience. It is possible to find a point for any object through which the entire weight of the object may be considered to act. This point is

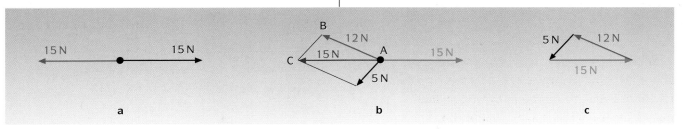

● *Figure 4.1* Equilibrium of  **a**  two and  **b**, **c**  three forces.

called the **centre of gravity** of the object. The weight does *not* act through the centre of gravity, but if it is assumed to act there then it can be shown that the same mathematical result is obtained as would be obtained if all the individual particles of the object were considered separately. In the case of many regular objects, a sphere for example, the centre of gravity of the object is at its centre.

## Turning effects of forces

The simple action of shutting a door uses a force to cause a rotation. Because the door is hinged, one edge of it will not move, so when a force is applied perpendicularly to the opposite edge the door closes. The effect on the door depends not only on the size of the force but also on how far from the hinge the force is applied and also at what angle the force is applied (*figures 4.3* and *4.4*). The turning effect of a force about a pivot is called its **moment** and is defined by the equation

moment of a force = force × perpendicular distance of pivot from the line of action of the force

This is illustrated in *figure 4.5*. In the simple case, *figure 4.5a*, the moment of the force is $F_1x_1$; in *figure 4.5b* be careful to note how $x_2$ is measured. The moment in this case is $F_2x_2$. The unit of the moment of a force is the newton metre (Nm), since it is a force multiplied by a distance. The **principle of moments** states that: for any object that is in equilibrium, the sum of the clockwise moments about any point provided by the forces acting on the object equals the sum of the anticlockwise moments about that point.

This is shown in the following example, which illustrates, in a simplified way, how the principle of moments can be used by structural engineers to determine the necessary strength and stability of any structure.

The oil platform, shown in *figure 4.6*, has a weight of $1.6 \times 10^6$N. It supports an oil-rig of weight $2.0 \times 10^5$N, a crane of weight $3.0 \times 10^5$N and the crane's load of $5.0 \times 10^4$N. The platform itself is supported on two legs at X and Y. The weights are shown acting through the centres of gravity of each item on the platform, and the horizontal distances between these weights are also given. Find the values of the two necessary support forces $S_1$ and $S_2$.

While it is possible to take moments about any point, it simplifies the problem to take moments about a point through which one of the unknown forces acts. In this case, therefore, take moments about X:

● **Figure 4.3** In a water wheel the weight of the water as it fills up each 'bucket' produces a moment that turns the wheel.

● **Figure 4.4** A mechanic uses a wrench because the long arm increases the moment that can be applied, which makes it easier to turn.

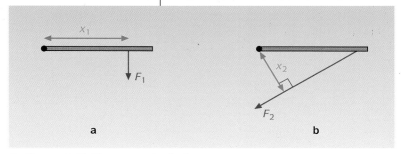

a                                                   b

● **Figure 4.5** The moment of a force.

clockwise moment of weight of oil-rig
$$= 2.0 \times 10^5 \text{N} \times 10.0 \text{m} = 2.0 \times 10^6 \text{Nm}$$
clockwise moment of weight of platform
$$= 1.6 \times 10^6 \text{N} \times 8.0 \text{m} = 12.8 \times 10^6 \text{Nm}$$
clockwise moment of weight of crane
$$= 3.0 \times 10^5 \text{N} \times 20.0 \text{m} = 6.0 \times 10^6 \text{Nm}$$
clockwise moment of weight of crane's load
$$= 5.0 \times 10^4 \text{N} \times 34.0 \text{m} = 1.7 \times 10^6 \text{Nm}$$

sum of clockwise moments $= 22.5 \times 10^6 \text{Nm}$

The sum of the anticlockwise moments must also be $22.5 \times 10^6 \text{Nm}$ and this is $S_2 \times 16 \text{m}$. Therefore

$$22.5 \times 10^6 = S_2 \times 16$$
$$S_2 = 1.41 \times 10^6 \text{N}$$

This somewhat lengthy process could be repeated by taking moments about Y, in order to find $S_1$, but it is simpler to use the fact that the sum of the upward forces must equal the sum of the downward forces if the object is in equilibrium. So

$$S_1 + S_2 = (2.0 \times 10^5) + (1.6 \times 10^6) +$$
$$(3.0 \times 10^5) + (5.0 \times 10^4) \text{N}$$
$$= 2.15 \times 10^6 \text{N}$$

Hence

$$S_1 = (2.15 \times 10^6 - 1.41 \times 10^6) \text{N} = 0.74 \times 10^6 \text{N}$$

# Torque

If two equal and opposite forces act on a body, the resultant force on the body is zero and so it will not accelerate. This was shown in *figure 4.1a*. However, on objects other than point objects, the two forces may act along different lines and, if they do, then, although the body will not accelerate, it will rotate. A familiar example of this is shown in the diagram of a steering wheel *(figure 4.7)*, where forces of 15 N are applied to the steering wheel in opposite directions. A pair of equal and opposite forces such as this is called a **couple**, and the turning effect that they cause is called a **torque**. To calculate the torque of the couple *(figure 4.7)*, the moment, in this case the clockwise moment, of each force is added together to get

$$(15 \text{N} \times 0.20 \text{m}) + (15 \text{N} \times 0.20 \text{m}) = 6 \text{Nm}$$

This can equally well be calculated by multiplying $15 \text{N} \times 0.40 \text{m} = 6 \text{Nm}$, showing that

torque of a couple = one of the forces × perpendicular distance between the forces

Complete equilibrium of a body is achieved when the resultant force and the resultant torque on the body are *both* zero.

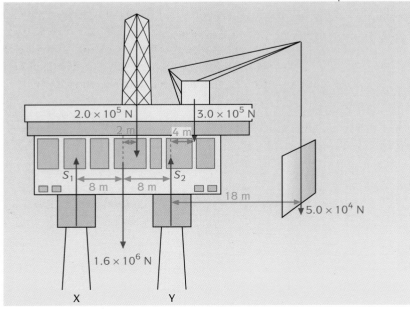

● *Figure 4.6*

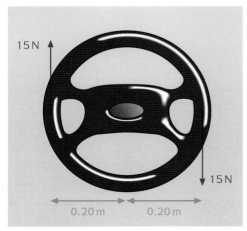

● *Figure 4.7*

## SAQ 4.2

A wheelbarrow is loaded as shown in *figure 4.9*. Calculate the force that the gardener needs to exert to hold the legs off the ground. What force is exerted by the ground on the legs of the wheelbarrow (taken both together) when the gardener is not holding the handles?

## SAQ 4.3

An old-fashioned pair of scales uses sliding masses of 10 g and 100 g to achieve a balance. A diagram of the arrangement is shown in *figure 4.10* and the bar itself is supported with its centre of gravity at the pivot. Calculate the value of the mass $M$, attached at X. What was the advantage of this method of weighing objects?

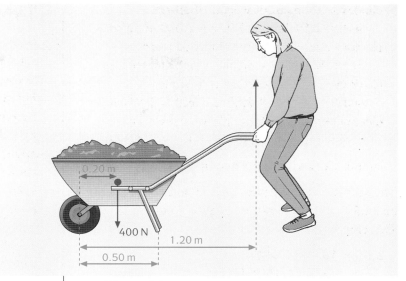

● *Figure 4.9*

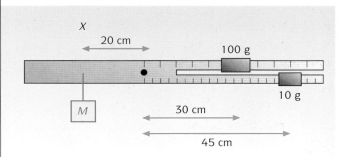

● *Figure 4.10*

● *Figure 4.8* The steering wheels of **a** a family saloon car and **b** a racing car. The same couple applied to each wheel produces more torque for **a** than for **b**, because **a** has a larger diameter. This makes a racing car much more difficult to drive.

## SAQ 4.4

The asymmetric bar shown in *figure 4.11* has a weight of 7.6 N and a centre of gravity that is 0.040 m from an end on which there is a load of 3.3 N. It is pivoted a distance of 0.060 m from its centre of gravity. Calculate the force $P$ that is necessary at the far end of the bar in order to maintain equilibrium.

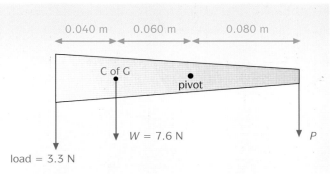

● *Figure 4.11*

## SAQ 4.5

A cantilevered balcony is shown in *figure 4.12*. Using the data given on the diagram, calculate the value of the support force *S*.

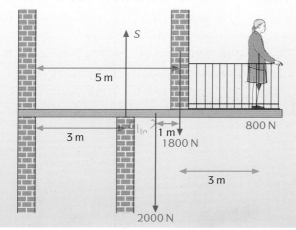

● **Figure 4.12**

## SUMMARY

■ The triangle of forces: if three forces are acting on a point object that is in equilibrium, they can be represented in magnitude and direction by the sides of a triangle taken in order.

■ The centre of gravity of an object is that point through which the entire weight of the object may be considered to act.

■ The moment of a force = force × perpendicular distance of the pivot from the line of action of the force.

■ The principle of moments: for any object that is in equilibrium, the sum of the clockwise moments about a point is equal to the sum of the anticlockwise moments about that same point.

■ A pair of equal and opposite forces, not acting in the same straight line, is called a *couple*, and the turning effect that they cause is called a *torque*.

■ The torque of a couple = one of the forces × perpendicular distance between the forces.

■ Equilibrium of a body is achieved when the resultant force and the resultant torque on the body are both zero.

## SAQ 4.6

The driving wheel of a car travelling at a constant velocity has a torque of 137 Nm applied to it by the axle that drives the car *(figure 4.13)*. The radius of the tyre is 0.18 m. What is the driving force provided by this wheel?

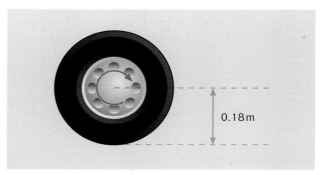

● **Figure 4.13**

## Question

1 A parascender of weight 440 N is being towed at a constant velocity by a rope which makes an angle of 25° to the horizontal. The parachute acts to provide a force on the parascender at an angle of 36° to the vertical, as shown in *figure 4.14*. Draw a triangle of forces to scale showing the direction of each force and also showing that the three forces acting on the person are 440 N, 530 N and 820 N. Which force is provided by the rope and which by the parachute?

Discuss qualitatively what is likely to happen to each of the three forces if the boat speeds up.

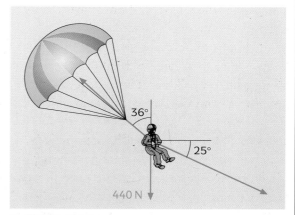

● **Figure 4.14**

# Work, energy and power

## Work

When a force moves in the direction of the force, work has to be done. **Work** is defined by the equation

work = force × displacement in the direction of the force

The unit of work is the joule (J). One joule is the work done when a force of one newton moves one metre in the direction of the force.

The implication of the definition of work is that the existence of a force by itself does not require work to be done. When a lift motor raises a lift containing some passengers, some work is done on the passengers because a force is exerted upwards on them and they move a distance upwards. If, for example, a particular passenger has a force of 650 N exerted on him and the distance he rises is 12 m, then the work done on him is 650 N × 12 m = 7800 J. No work is done if the lift does not move. The floor the passenger steps out on to does not do work on the passenger even though it exerts a force on him. Note that this will not be the case if you have to use your muscles to exert a force that does not move. This is because the behaviour of muscles when exerting a force does result in movement within the muscle fibres, so you get tired because work is being done within the muscle (*figure 5.1*).

## Energy

In order to do work, energy must be used. **Energy** can be defined by the statement: energy is the stored ability to do work.

Energy may be stored in all sorts of different forms, and there are occasions when it is difficult to be precise about the exact form in which the energy is stored. It is stored in mechanical form as potential energy in the water in a lake high up above a hydro-electricity station (*figure 5.2*) or as kinetic energy in a moving train. It is stored in

● *Figure 5.1* A weight-lifter does work even when the bar is held stationary above the head, because the muscles are constantly moving internally.

● *Figure 5.2* A hydro-electric power station uses the gravitational potential energy of water, stored above sea-level by a dam, to generate electrical energy.

chemical form as chemical energy in fuels such as oil and coal *(figure 5.3)*, and in food, but in these cases it is necessary to consider the oxygen with which the fuels react when making any calculations about the quantity of energy stored. At an atomic level, it is stored in the movement of individual atoms and molecules in a form of energy called **internal energy**. This illustrates the difficulty, as internal energy is the sum of the kinetic and potential energies of all the atoms within a body. Releasing energy from these different stores can be difficult and is often inefficient, but the fact that the energy can be used to do work implies that energy, as well as work, is measured in joules.

The relationship between energy and work is important. It is sometimes helpful to think of the two terms in much the same way as credits and debits are used with a bank account. Energy is a

credit: it is stored ready for the time when it is used to do work; the account is then debited by the amount of work done. When this work is done on some object, then that object will gain a corresponding amount of energy. The law that generalises this is known as the **law of conservation of energy**. It states that: energy cannot be created or destroyed but may be converted from one form into another.

In some respects this law seems to contradict common sense. The people of the Earth are using up fossil fuels at a rapid rate *(figure 5.4)*. The energy that has been stored for millions of years in these fuels and the oxygen with which they combine is converted to chemical form. We use the energy for heating our homes, for driving our cars, for providing electricity from power stations. This causes a rise in the temperature of the Earth, and the law implies that the loss of energy from the fossil fuels when they react with the oxygen in the atmosphere equals the energy gained by the Earth and its atmosphere. This energy is in the form of the internal energy of the molecules of the Earth and its atmosphere. However, the Earth radiates energy out into space in the form of infrared radiation. To all intents and purposes, therefore, it is lost to us for ever. The store of fossil fuels is certainly being depleted and will be exhausted some time in the future if we continue to use it at the present rate. Of course, the economics of the situation are also important and, as the store of fossil fuels diminishes, their price will rise. A point will be reached at which it becomes more economical

● *Figure 5.3* Burning coal converts chemical energy to heat energy.

● *Figure 5.4* Many millions of kilograms of coal are used in the power stations of Britain every day.

to use renewable energy, such as the infrared energy from the Sun *(figure 5.5)*. At present we are wasteful with energy from fossil fuels because it is cheap and plentiful.

## Gravitational potential energy

When an object is lifted, work is done on it to move it against the force of gravity. The object gains gravitational potential energy as a result of this; that is, it can do work against something else when it comes back down. There are other forms of potential energy such as elastic potential energy and electrical potential energy, so it is preferable to use the full term 'gravitational potential energy' rather than its abbreviated form 'potential energy'.

The use of the quantity 'gravitational potential energy' is illustrated by the following example.

A crane lifts a 500 kg load a distance of 16.0 m at a constant speed. Since the speed is constant, the upward force that the cable exerts on the load is equal to the weight of the load. The following information is available:

weight of load $= 500 \, \text{kg} \times 9.8 \, \text{N} \, \text{kg}^{-1}$
upward force of cable on load
$= 500 \, \text{kg} \times 9.8 \, \text{N} \, \text{kg}^{-1}$

**● Figure 5.5** The Sun emits vast quantities of energy converted from nuclear energy.

work done by cable on load
$= 500 \, \text{kg} \times 9.8 \, \text{N} \, \text{kg}^{-1} \times 16.0 \, \text{m} = 78 \, 400 \, \text{J}$
gain in gravitational potential energy of load
$= 78 \, 400 \, \text{J}$

The gravitational potential energy of this load could be used to do work.

The example shows that the gain in the **gravitational potential energy** of a body can be obtained by using the following equation:

gain in gravitational potential energy
$= $ mass $\times g \times$ vertical displacement moved

i.e. gravitational potential energy $= mgh$

## Kinetic energy

An object that is moving stores energy as kinetic energy. In order to find out how much energy is stored in this form, consider the following example.

A person of mass 62 kg on a bicycle of mass 8 kg is travelling with speed 10 m s$^{-1}$. In order to stop, the cyclist applies the brakes so that a stopping force of 500 N is applied to the bicycle. This means that work is done by the bicycle against the stopping force. The amount of work done must equal the kinetic energy of the bicycle and cyclist. First, it is necessary to calculate the (negative) acceleration of the cyclist so that the distance travelled while braking can be found. Since

$$\text{force} = \text{mass} \times \text{acceleration}$$
$$-500 \, \text{N} = (62 + 8) \, \text{kg} \times \text{acceleration}$$
$$\text{acceleration} = -\frac{500}{70} \, \text{m} \, \text{s}^{-2}$$

Also $v^2 = u^2 + 2as$, so

$$0 = 10^2 + 2 \left( -\frac{500}{70} \right) s$$
$$s = \frac{10^2 \times 70}{2 \times 500}$$

The work done is

$$F \times s = 500 \times \frac{10^2 \times 70}{2 \times 500} = 3500 \, \text{J}$$

If the numbers here are inspected, it will be seen that the figure of 500 N cancels out. In other words it does not matter what the stopping force is, the kinetic energy is 3500 J. It can also be seen that work done = kinetic energy before braking

$$= \frac{10^2 \times 70}{2} = \frac{u^2 \times m}{2}$$

This is a statement that you need to know in the following form. A body of mass $m$ travelling with velocity of magnitude $v$ has **kinetic energy** given by

$$\text{kinetic energy} = \tfrac{1}{2}mv^2$$

We now consider another example. Find the kinetic energy of a person of mass 60 kg who is travelling at 70 m s$^{-1}$ when in a plane that is just touching down on a runway. What force is needed to stop the person in a distance of (a) 2100 m, (b) 700 m?

The kinetic energy of the person is

$$\tfrac{1}{2}mv^2 = \tfrac{1}{2} \times 60\,\text{kg} \times (70\,\text{m s}^{-1})^2 = 147\,000\,\text{J}$$

This energy is used to do work against the braking force $F$, which, for a person, is provided by the seat belt and the seat. So for (a)

$$147\,000\,\text{J} = F \times 2100\,\text{m}$$
$$F = 147\,000/2100 = 70\,\text{N}$$

and for (b)

$$147\,000\,\text{J} = F \times 700\,\text{m}$$
$$F = 210\,\text{N}$$

Note that, as the distance for stopping decreases, the force required for stopping increases. This has important implications for accidents. The most dangerous accidents are those in which sudden stops take place. The designers of all modes of transport try to design systems that allow greater distances for stopping in an emergency.

### SAQ 5.1
How much gravitational potential energy is gained if you climb a flight of stairs? Assume that you have a mass of 52 kg and that the height you lift yourself is 2.5 m.

### SAQ 5.2
How much gravitational potential energy is lost by an aircraft of mass 80 000 kg if it descends from an altitude of 10 000 m to an altitude of 1000 m? What happens to this energy if the pilot keeps the speed of the plane constant?

● *Figure 5.6* A high dive is an example of converting gravitational potential energy to kinetic energy. Into what forms of energy might this kinetic energy be converted when the diver enters the water?

### SAQ 5.3
Calculate the change in kinetic energy of a ball of mass 200 g when it bounces. Assume that it hits the ground with a speed of 15.8 m s$^{-1}$ and leaves it at 12.2 m s$^{-1}$.

### SAQ 5.4
Calculate the gravitational potential energy of a high diver if she has a mass of 45 kg and her centre of gravity is 5.0 m above the water. Assuming that all her gravitational potential energy becomes kinetic energy during the dive, calculate her velocity as she enters the water *(figure 5.6)*.

### SAQ 5.5
A car of mass 800 kg is travelling at 35 m s$^{-1}$; a van of mass 2000 kg is travelling at 20 m s$^{-1}$. Copy and complete the following table showing both the momentum and the kinetic energy for each vehicle and comment on the relative sizes of your answers.

|  | *Car* | *Van* |
|---|---|---|
| Momentum |  |  |
| Kinetic energy |  |  |

## Elastic and inelastic collisions

As explained in chapter 3, in *any* collision, momentum is conserved. Kinetic energy, however, is not usually conserved; the fact that you can hear many collisions must imply that some sound energy is emitted, and in many collisions a great deal of thermal energy is generated. If a collision is called an **elastic collision** then no kinetic energy is converted to other forms. **Inelastic collisions**, the vast majority, are those in which kinetic energy is converted to other forms. (Be careful with the terminology here. You will sometimes see *perfectly elastic* collisions referred to. This implies no change in total kinetic energy. Sometimes *perfectly inelastic* is the term used. This implies that the two colliding objects stick together, and if one of them is the ground then no bouncing takes place.)

The mathematics of elastic collisions occurring in a straight line is interesting. Consider the situation shown in *figure 5.7*. An object of mass $M$ travelling with velocity $U$ is catching up, and then collides elastically and head on, with an object of mass $m$ travelling with velocity $u$. After the collision the two objects continue to move in the same straight line with velocities of $V$ and $v$ respectively. An elastic collision such as this may be thought of as a collision between two molecules of a gas.

First, apply the law of conservation of momentum to the collision:

$$MU + mu = MV + mv$$

Also, since total kinetic energy is unchanged in an elastic collision, we get

$$\tfrac{1}{2}MU^2 + \tfrac{1}{2}mu^2 = \tfrac{1}{2}MV^2 + \tfrac{1}{2}mv^2$$

Cancelling the $\tfrac{1}{2}$ gives

$$MU^2 + mu^2 = MV^2 + mv^2$$

The kinetic energy and momentum equations are deceptively similar. They can be simplified if, for both equations, $M$ is put on one side of the equation and $m$ is put on the other. This gives

$$MU^2 - MV^2 = mv^2 - mu^2$$

and

$$MU - MV = mv - mu$$

These two equations can then be divided by one another to eliminate both $M$ and $m$:

$$\frac{MU^2 - MV^2}{MU - MV} = \frac{mv^2 - mu^2}{mv - mu}$$

$$\frac{U^2 - V^2}{U - V} = \frac{v^2 - u^2}{v - u}$$

or

$$\frac{(U - V)(U + V)}{(U - V)} = \frac{(v - u)(v + u)}{(v - u)}$$

and further cancelling gives

$$U + V = v + u$$

or

$$U - u = v - V$$

Since $U - u$ is the **relative velocity** of approach between the two objects, and $v - V$ is the relative velocity of separation after the collision, this lengthy piece of mathematics shows that, for an elastic collision

the relative velocity of approach
= the relative velocity of separation

This equation can be used in practical situations such as that given in the following example, which is important in the behaviour of the moderator in a nuclear reactor.

A neutron, of mass 1 atomic mass unit, collides head on with a stationary carbon atom, of mass 12 atomic mass units. What fraction of its kinetic energy is retained by the neutron after the collision? Note that the rest of

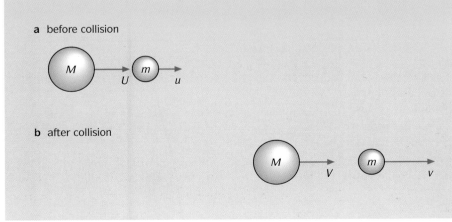

**a** before collision

$M$   $U$   $m$   $u$

**b** after collision

$M$   $V$   $m$   $v$

● *Figure 5.7* Elastic collision in a straight line.

the kinetic energy will be transferred to the carbon atom.

Let the initial velocity of the neutron be *u*. Using the same terminology as that shown in *figure 5.7* we get: from the conservation of momentum,

$$mu = mv + MV$$
$$(1 \times u) = (1 \times v) + (12 \times V) \qquad \text{(a)}$$

(the conversion factor from atomic mass units into kilograms conveniently cancels out) and from the relative velocity of approach equals the relative velocity of separation,

$$u = (V - v) \qquad \text{so} \qquad V = u + v \qquad \text{(b)}$$

Combining (a) and (b) to eliminate *V* gives

$$u = v + 12(u + v)$$
$$-11u = 13v$$

so

$$\frac{v}{u} = -\frac{11}{13}$$

(The minus sign indicates that the neutron bounces back off the carbon atom.) This gives the fraction of kinetic energy retained by the neutron as

$$\frac{\frac{1}{2}mv^2}{\frac{1}{2}mu^2} = \frac{v^2}{u^2} = \frac{11^2}{13^2} = 0.72$$

### SAQ 5.6

What fraction of the kinetic energy is retained by a neutron when it collides elastically with a uranium atom of mass 238 atomic mass units? (This question is similar to the example given above.)

### SAQ 5.7

When a stationary radioactive atom of mass 238 atomic mass units undergoes radioactive decay it emits an α-particle (alpha-particle) of mass 4 atomic mass units. Assuming that all the energy released is in the form of the kinetic energies of the α-particle and the recoil atom, calculate the fraction of the total energy released by the decay that is stored as the kinetic energy of the α-particle.

# Energy transfers

*Table 5.1* gives some practical situations in which energy is used to do work. The numbers must be treated as a guide rather than being exact. They show great differences between the different transfers. The theoretical values, quoted in some cases, have been found by making certain basic assumptions. Note that in the cases of all the engines quoted it is necessary to state the temperature of the gas that drives the engine. In the case of the steam engine *(figure 5.8)*, for example, this is taken to be steam at 100 °C.

● *Figure 5.8* A steam engine has a very low efficiency.

| Situation | Type of energy used | Percentage of stored energy that may be used to do work in | |
|---|---|---|---|
| | | theory | practice |
| Hydro-electric power | gravitational potential | 100 | 90 |
| Car diesel engine | internal energy of gas at 1500 K | 80 | 50 |
| Car petrol engine | internal energy of gas at 900 K | 70 | 40 |
| Power station | internal energy of gas at 900 K | 70 | 40 |
| Car battery | chemical | – | 25 |
| Steam engine | internal energy of gas at 373 K | 25 | 5 |
| Photosynthesis | light | 18 | 5 |
| Microphone | sound | – | 2 |

● *Table 5.1* Energy is used to do work in various situations

# Power

**Power** is the rate of doing work. It is therefore also the rate at which energy is transferred. In equation form this is:

average power = work done/time taken

The unit of power is the watt (W). One watt is one joule per second.

Power may also be expressed by putting the work done as the force × the distance. This gives

$$\text{power} = \frac{\text{force} \times \text{distance}}{\text{time}} = \text{force} \times \frac{\text{distance}}{\text{time}}$$

$$= \text{force} \times \text{velocity}$$

# The kilowatt hour (kWh)

The joule is a rather small unit of energy for use domestically and commercially. For example, an electricity bill issued to a domestic consumer in 1994 and charging £100.00 for electrical energy would be charging for the supply of 4 500 000 000 joules of electrical energy. In order to elimininate such large numbers, the unit *kilowatt hour* is used (*figure 5.9*). Note: it is *not* a kilowatt *per* hour, it is a kilowatt *for* an hour. Since a watt is a joule per second, the kilowatt hour is therefore a supply of energy at a rate of 1000 joules each second for 3600 seconds; that is 1000 joules per second for 3600 seconds, a total energy supply of 3 600 000 J. So

1 kWh = 3 600 000 J

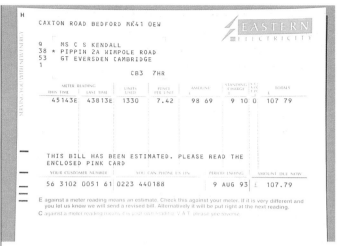

● **Figure 5.9** A typical domestic electricity bill. Note how the costs are calculated using the kilowatt hour as a unit of energy.

In the example given above, the householder would be charged £100.00 for

$$\frac{4\,500\,000\,000}{3\,600\,000} = 1250\,\text{kWh}$$

This is a typical cost of electrical energy at 8 p per kWh.

*Table 5.2* shows how to estimate the cost of the electrical energy supplied each day to a household. The values it uses should only be thought of as a guide, but the table does show how expensive some items are to use and how cheap are some others. This total cost is for one day, so an electricity bill, which is usually prepared every three months, would come to over £200.00 once overhead charges and VAT are added.

| Appliance | Power/kW | Time used/h | Energy/kWh | Cost/pence |
|---|---|---|---|---|
| Television | 0.200 | 4.0 | 0.80 | 6.4 |
| Water heater | 3.00 | 2.0 | 6.0 | 48.0 |
| Hair drier | 1.30 | 0.2 | 0.26 | 2.1 |
| Hi-fi | 0.090 | 2.0 | 0.18 | 1.4 |
| Dishwasher | 2.00 | 1.0 | 2.0 | 16.0 |
| Deep freeze | 0.40 | 10.0 | 4.0 | 32.0 |
| Fridge | 0.15 | 10.0 | 1.5 | 12.0 |
| Lights | 0.10 | 30.0 | 3.0 | 24.0 |
| Lights | 0.060 | 20.0 | 1.2 | 9.6 |
| | | | | 151.5 |
| Total | | | | (£1.51) |

● **Table 5.2** Estimated cost of household electricity

## Safety note

There are three potential hazards that may arise from the use of batteries. First, a rechargeable battery may have a very low internal resistance. Its terminals should **never be directly connected** by a wire, as there could then be such a large current that the wire would overheat and burn the plastic insulation. Secondly, lead–acid batteries, such as those used in cars, give off hydrogen gas when they are being charged. Hydrogen is flammable, so **no naked flame** should be used in the vicinity of a charging battery and any experiment should not be carried out in a confined space. Thirdly, lead-acid batteries contain corrosive acid, so **laboratory coats and goggles** should be worn.

## Experiment to find the efficiency of a battery

One of the figures quoted as an example in *table 5.1* can be obtained experimentally. If an initially discharged car battery, or other rechargeable battery, is charged for a suitable time, the energy supplied to it can be measured.

If then the energy delivered from it on total discharge is measured, the efficiency of the battery can be obtained from the equation

efficiency

$$= \frac{\text{energy delivered by the battery during discharge}}{\text{energy supplied to the battery during charge}}$$

Design an electrical circuit that will enable you to measure these quantities (see chapter 7). You may be able to use an energy meter, but, if not, use an ammeter and voltmeter to enable you to plot graphs of power supplied against time and power delivered against time. The graphs, which will not be straight-line graphs, can then be used to find the total energy supplied and the total energy delivered.

● *Figure 5.10* A gear-box is an extremely important part in many mechanical devices. The torque an engine delivers can be varied only within narrow limits, so a gear-box is used to adapt the driving forces applied to the varying external conditions.

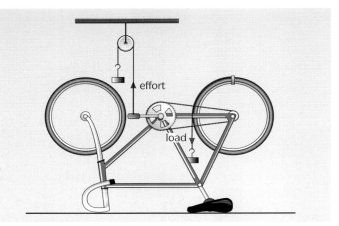

● *Figure 5.11* A method for measuring efficiency.

## Experiment to find the efficiency of gears

A gear-box is a device that is attached to an engine in order to change the rate at which a drive-shaft rotates *(figure 5.10)*. For example, a car engine may turn the gear wheel at the front of the gear-box at a rate of 2400 revolutions per minute (2400 rpm). The drive-shaft from the back of the gear-box may rotate at 2400 rpm, 1600 rpm, 1200 rpm or 800 rpm depending what gear the driver is in.

The efficiency of a gear-box is given by

$$\text{efficiency} = \frac{\text{energy delivered by the gear-box}}{\text{energy supplied to the gear-box}}$$

Note that, since in this case the time during which the energy is delivered is equal to the time during which the energy is supplied, it is equally possible to write

$$\text{efficiency} = \frac{\text{power delivered by the gear-box}}{\text{power supplied to the gear-box}}$$

Design and carry out an experiment to measure the efficiency of a gear system. Possible gear systems that you can use are a car or motorcycle gear-box, a model gear system such as Techtronix or Lego, or a bicycle. A suggestion for finding the efficiency of a bicycle is illustrated in *figure 5.11*. The efficiency will vary with the gear the bicycle is in. You will need to measure what effort is needed to move a particular load. After you have found this, you will also need to find how many revolutions of the back wheel take place for one revolution of the pedals. It is standard practice when this type of information is required to measure the number of turns of the back wheel for, say, 50 turns of the pedals, and then to divide by 50. The circumference of the back wheel and the circumference of the circle through which the pedals turn will also be needed (although a short cut can be made use of here in which only the two radii are required.)

## Experiment to investigate momentum and energy

Design and carry out an investigation to find how the mass of a golf club affects the speed of a golf ball. You do not need to use a real golf club, since it is difficult to alter its mass, but an arrangement such as that shown in *figure 5.12* may be considered. If the block is always released from a given height, then the speed of the block when it reaches the golf ball will be the same, whatever mass rests on the block. (Why is this?) The speed of the ball after it has been struck by the block may be determined in a variety of ways. You may consider that a ticker-tape method is appropriate, or be able to use a strobe light or a photodiode and an electronic clock or, more simply, measure the distance from the tee to the point at which the ball hits the ground.

What is the maximum speed of the ball, in terms of the speed of the block?

There are several other investigations that you could do with similar apparatus. For example, if the block and the ball are covered with electrically conducting paint, an electronic timer can be used to determine the contact time between the ball and the block. This, too, will vary with the mass of the block. Another possibility is to vary the speed of the block, but changing too many factors at once will complicate things. The general rule is to change only one quantity at a time and to find the effect that this has on one other quantity.

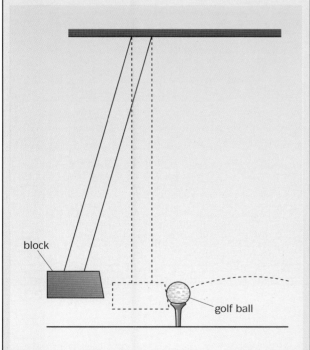

● *Figure 5.12* Investigating momentum and energy by simulating the action of a golf club.

block

golf ball

### SAQ 5.8

Calculate the power that needs to be supplied by an electric motor if a load of 3000 N is to be lifted a distance of 20 m in 25 s.

### SAQ 5.9

What power is being used by a microwave oven if 0.16 kWh of energy are used in 16 minutes?

### SAQ 5.10

A lorry of total mass 35 000 kg is climbing a hill with a gradient of 8% at a constant speed of 13 m s$^{-1}$. The driving force that is exerted on it is 40 000 N. Calculate
**a** the useful power which the engine is developing, and
**b** the fraction of this power that is being changed into gravitational potential energy per unit time. What happens to the rest of the power that the lorry develops?

# SUMMARY

- ■ Work = force × distance moved in direction of force.
- ■ Energy is the stored ability to do work.
- ■ Gain in gravitational potential energy
  = mass × *g* × vertical displacement = *mgh*.
- ■ Kinetic energy = $\frac{1}{2}$ × mass × velocity$^2$ = $\frac{1}{2}mv^2$.
- ■ In an elastic collision, no kinetic energy is converted to other forms; in an inelastic collision, there is a conversion of kinetic energy.
- ■ For a totally elastic collision, the relative velocity of approach = the relative velocity of separation.
- ■ Power is the rate of doing work; it is the rate at which energy is transferred:

$$\text{power} = \frac{\text{work done}}{\text{time}} = \text{force} \times \text{velocity}.$$

- ■ The law of conservation of energy states that: energy cannot be created or destroyed but may be converted from one form into another.
- ■ Efficiency of a system

$$= \frac{\text{energy from the system}}{\text{energy supplied to the system}}$$

$$= \frac{\text{power from the system}}{\text{power supplied to the system}}.$$

- ■ The kilowatt hour is a convenient unit of energy, equal to a power of 1 kW being used for 1 h.
  1 kWh = 3 600 000 J.

## Questions

1  A long jumper has a mass of 70 kg and, at take-off, a velocity of $9.0\,\mathrm{m\,s^{-1}}$ in a direction at 30° to the ground.
   Calculate the following.
   a  The kinetic energy of the athlete at take-off.
   b  The momentum of the athlete at take-off.
   c  The vertical component of the take-off velocity.
   d  The time the athlete is in the air.
   e  The horizontal component of the take-off velocity.
   f  The length of the jump.
   Explain **two** ways in which the athlete could increase the length of the jump.

2  The engine of a train has a useful power output of 400 kW and it is pulling the train at a speed of $60\,\mathrm{m\,s^{-1}}$.
   The total mass of the engine and train is 600 tonnes ($6.0 \times 10^5\,\mathrm{kg}$).
   a  Calculate the kinetic energy and the momentum of the train.
   b  Calculate the driving force that the engine is exerting.

# *Waves*

## Vibrations

A vibration or oscillation is simply a wobble! An object or particle is vibrating when it moves backwards and forwards about a fixed point. You may have met many examples of vibrations in your life, such as:

■ air moving from a loudspeaker;
■ a ruler being twanged over the edge of a bench;
■ the string on a guitar or violin;
■ a car or bike vibrating when it goes over a bumpy road;
■ a shock wave through the ground produced by an explosion;
■ quartz crystals used in watches;
■ the electrical signal in an alternating current;
■ water particles in a sea wave.

When a string of a guitar vibrates, a wave is formed, and this is also true for the other vibrations. In fact, all vibrations produce waves of one type or another *(figure 6.1)*. Waves that move through a material (or a vacuum) are called **progressive waves**.

You need to know the following important definitions about waves and wave motion *(figure 6.2)*:

■ The number of vibrations per second of any vibrating system is called its **frequency** ($f$). The higher the frequency of a musical note, the higher its pitch. Frequency is measured in hertz (Hz), where 1 Hz = one vibration per second (1 kHz = $10^3$ Hz and 1 megahertz (MHz) = $10^6$ Hz).

■ The distance from any point on a wave to another exactly similar point (e.g. crest to crest) is called the **wavelength** ($\lambda$, the Greek letter 'lambda' ) (usually measured in metres).

■ The distance of a point on the wave from its undisturbed position is called the **displacement** ($x$) and is also measured in metres.

● *Figure 6.1* Radio telescopes detect radio waves from distant stars, and a rainbow is an effect caused by the refraction of light waves by water droplets.

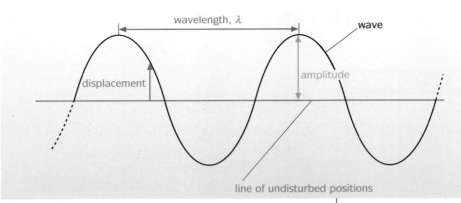

● **Figure 6.2** A wave, showing some of the terms used.

■ The maximum displacement of any point on the wave from its undisturbed position is called the **amplitude** (also measured in metres). The greater the amplitude of the vibration, the louder the sound or the rougher the sea!

■ The natural rate of vibration of an object depends on a number of things. Small, light and stiff objects naturally vibrate with a high frequency, while large, heavy and slack objects vibrate with a low frequency.

■ The time taken for one complete vibration is called the **period** of the motion ($T$). It is measured in seconds and is the inverse of the frequency, i.e. $T = 1/f$.

Waves are called mechanical waves if the waves need a substance (medium) through which to travel. Sound is one example of such a wave. Other cases are waves on springs, strings and water waves *(figure 6.3)*. Some properties of these waves are given later (see page 52).

● **Figure 6.3** The impact of a droplet on the surface of a liquid creates a vibration, which in turn gives rise to waves on the surface.

The vibrations producing mechanical waves are of two distinct types, longitudinal and transverse. Longitudinal vibrations give **longitudinal waves**, where the particles vibrating are moving backwards and forwards along the direction of wave motion *(figure 6.4a)* – sound waves are an example of this type . Transverse vibrations give **transverse waves**, where the particles are moving at right-angles to the direction of wave motion *(figure 6.4b)* – surface water waves are an example of this type.

A very simple method of showing the difference between these two wave types is to use a slinky spring. Vibrating it sideways gives a transverse wave while vibrating one end backwards and forwards produces a longitudinal wave.

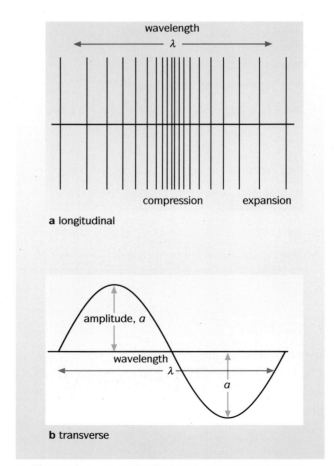

● **Figure 6.4** **a** Longitudinal and **b** transverse waves.

## Longitudinal waves

In the apparatus shown in *figure* 6.5 the oscillator is connected to one end of the slinky. When it is switched on, the end of the slinky is moved up and down, and a series of longitudinal pulses travel up the slinky and reflect from the top.

You can use the apparatus shown in *figure* 6.6 to measure the velocity of a longitudinal compression pulse (wave) in the rod. (The hammer must hit the rod hard enough for it to move away from the hammer after collision.)

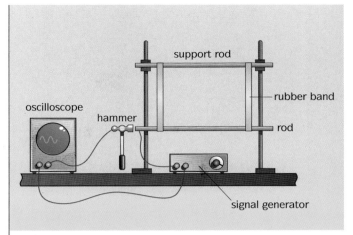

● *Figure 6.6* Measuring the velocity of a longitudinal wave pulse.

## Transverse waves

These can be demonstrated using the apparatus shown in *figure* 6.7. One end of a rubber cord is attached to a small weight that hangs over a pulley and the other end is fixed to an oscillator that vibrates in a vertical plane. The oscillator produces transverse oscillations at the end of the cord, so transverse waves travel down it. The shape of the waves depends on how the displacement of the oscillator output changes with time.

You can investigate the motion of a large loud-speaker at different frequencies using a stroboscope. An interesting extension of this experiment would be the study of the vibrations of a violin body when different notes are played on the strings.

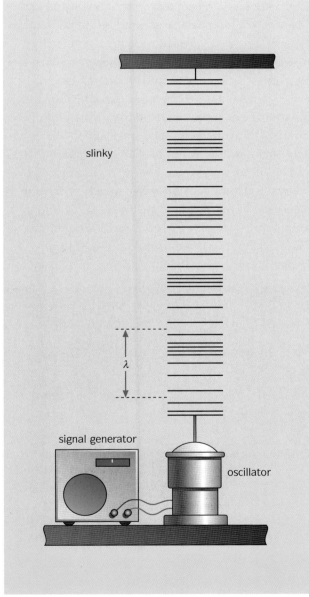

● *Figure 6.5* Making a longitudinal wave on a slinky using an oscillator.

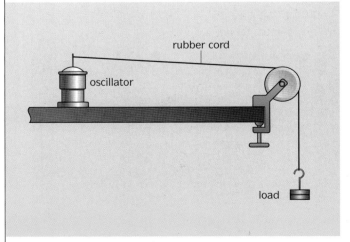

● *Figure 6.7* Making a transverse wave on a stretched rubber cord using an oscillator.

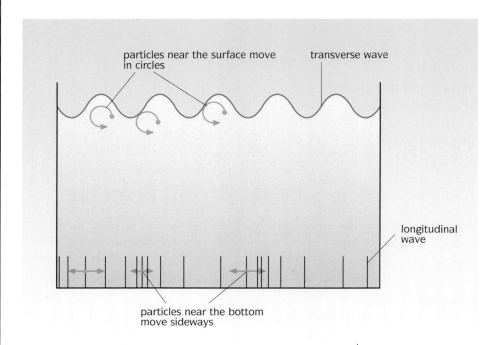

*Figure 6.8* Water waves in a tank.

Waves in water are quite complex. If water waves in a tank are viewed from the side, you can see that particles near the top move in circles, giving transverse waves on the water surface, while those near the bottom move backwards and forwards, giving a longitudinal wave motion *(figure 6.8)*.

## Wave energy

It is important to realise that, for both types of mechanical wave, the particles that make up the material through which the wave is travelling do not move along, they only oscillate about a fixed point. It is the *energy* that is transmitted by the wave. You can see this clearly by watching the effect of wind blowing in a cornfield. You notice a wave going across the field while the individual stalks remain in place *(figure 6.9)*.

The energy carried by a wave can be considerable. For example, the shock waves from the eruption of a volcano can cause serious structural damage over a wide area. The energy carried in such shock waves is of the order of $10^{20}$ J! (Remember that of Mount Pinatubo, which devastated parts of the Philippines in 1988.) Scientists produce small shock waves to help them in their study of the Earth *(figure 6.10)*.

The speed with which energy is transmitted by the wave is known as the **wave speed** ($v$). This is measured in $\text{m s}^{-1}$. The wave speed for sound in air at a pressure of $10^5 \text{ N m}^{-2}$ and a temperature of 273 K is about $330 \text{ m s}^{-1}$ while for light in a vacuum it is almost $300\,000\,000 \text{ m s}^{-1}$.

*Figure 6.10* Small shock waves are sent through the ground by machines like this one. The ways in which these seismic waves are reflected can be measured. Different types of rock and liquid produce different reflection patterns, which can help scientists to detect new supplies of oil and other natural resources.

*Figure 6.9* Wind causes waves in a cornfield.

## Phase, and phase difference

The **phase** of the wave motion at any point is related to the displacement of the wave at zero time. Any two points on the wave will have a **phase difference** between them, and this will be anything from 0° to 360° *(figure 6.11a)*.

A good example of phase difference is a pendulum swinging over a ball on a turntable *(figure 6.11b)*. If they are exactly in phase, the pendulum bob and the ball appear to stay one above the other when viewed from the side. If there is a phase difference between them, they are separated by a constant amount.

The phase difference between two electrical signals can be measured very easily using the apparatus shown in *figure 6.12a*. One of the signals is applied to the *x* plates of the oscilloscope (with the time base switched off) and the other is connected to the *y* plates. If they are exactly in phase (or out of phase by 180°), a straight line will be seen, while other phase differences will show an ellipse *(figure 6.12b)*, the inclination of the ellipse giving the phase difference.

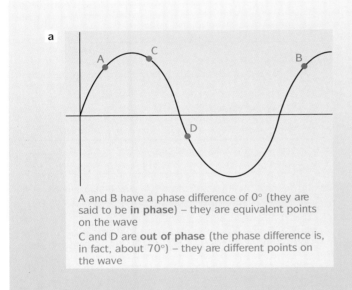 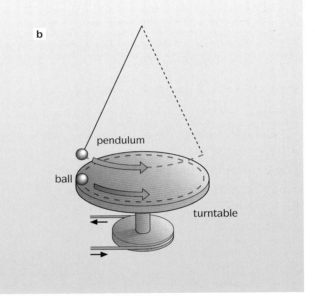

A and B have a phase difference of 0° (they are said to be **in phase**) – they are equivalent points on the wave

C and D are **out of phase** (the phase difference is, in fact, about 70°) – they are different points on the wave

● *Figure 6.11* Phase, and phase difference.

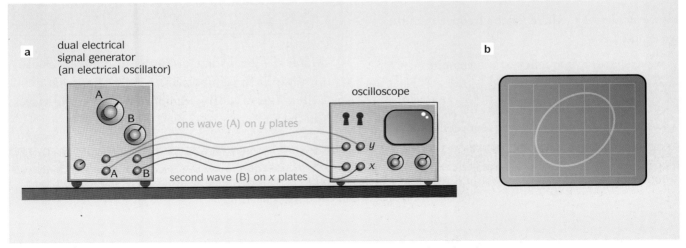

● *Figure 6.12* Apparatus to measure the phase difference between two electrical signals.

● *Figure 6.13* Each string in a piano produces a different note, because each is carefully tuned to produce a different frequency of sound wave.

## Wave equation

An important equation connecting some of the wave variables can be found as follows. You know that

$$\text{speed} = \frac{\text{distance}}{\text{time}}$$

But a wave will travel a distance of one wavelength in a time equal to one period ($T$). So

$$\text{wave speed} = \frac{\text{wavelength}}{\text{period}}$$

However, $T = 1/f$, where $f$ is the frequency of the wave and so

$$\text{wave speed} = \text{frequency} \times \text{wavelength}$$
$$v = f \times \lambda$$

Clearly, for a given speed of wave, the greater the wavelength, the smaller the frequency and vice versa.

We shall now work through an example. Middle C on a piano tuned to concert pitch should have a frequency of 264 Hz *(figure 6.13)*; if the speed of sound is $330\,\text{m s}^{-1}$, calculate the wavelength of the sound produced when this key is played. We use the above equation in slightly rewritten form:

$$\text{wavelength} = \frac{\text{speed}}{\text{frequency}}$$
$$= \frac{330\,\text{m s}^{-1}}{264\,\text{Hz}} = 1.25\,\text{m}$$

### SAQ 6.1

What is the frequency of a longitudinal vibration of wavelength 0.25 m that travels through steel at a speed of $5060\,\text{m s}^{-1}$?

### SAQ 6.2

A cello string vibrates with a frequency of 64 Hz. If the wavelength of the waves on the string is 180 cm, what is the wave speed?

### SAQ 6.3

Copy and complete the following table (you may assume that the speed of radio waves is $3 \times 10^{8}\,\text{m s}^{-1}$).

| Station | Wavelength, $\lambda$/m | Frequency, $f$/MHz |
|---|---|---|
| Radio 1 (FM) | | 97.6 |
| Radio 2 (FM) | | 90.2 |
| Radio 3 | | 92.4 |
| Radio 4 (FM) | | 94.6 |
| Radio 4 (LW) | 1500 | |
| Radio 5 | 693 | |

*Table 6.1* gives some properties of three mechanical waves. It is important to realise here that the vibrations of a string can produce the sound waves in the air.

| | Water waves | Sound waves in air | Waves on strings and springs |
|---|---|---|---|
| Frequency/Hz | about 6 | 20–20 000 (limits of human hearing) | about 2 |
| Speed/m s$^{-1}$ | about 0.12 | about 300 | about 1 |
| Wavelength/m | about 0.02 | 15 to 0.015 | about 0.5 |

● *Table 6.1* Properties of mechanical waves

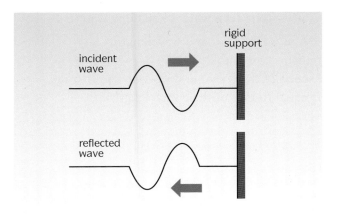

● *Figure 6.14* Phase change of a pulse on a cord reflected from a 'rigid' support.

# Reflection of waves

When the wave in the slinky hits the support in the experiments described on page 49, it is reflected. If the support is rigid, most of the energy in the incoming pulse will be transferred to the reflected pulse. This means that the velocity of the wave will be reversed, but its amplitude will be unchanged. The frequency will also stay the same; if it did not, the reflected sound from an orchestra would be of different pitch from the direct sound – and some very peculiar effects would result!

One thing that does change apart from the velocity is the phase of the pulse – this is shown in *figure 6.14*. The reflected pulse is exactly half a wavelength out of step with the incoming pulse. The reflected pulse is upside down. This means a phase change of 180°. It is very simple to show this

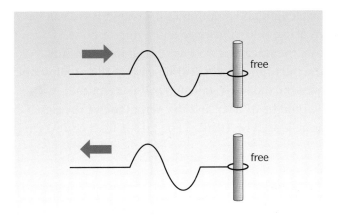

● *Figure 6.15* Reflection of a pulse on a cord from a 'free' end.

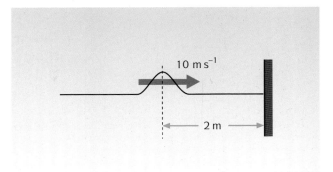

● *Figure 6.16* Wave on a rubber cord (see SAQ 6.4).

using a rubber cord fixed to a rigid support and stretched tight.

This is only true if the end is fixed. If the end of the cord is connected to a ring that is free to move up and down a vertical post, then the wave reflects in the way shown in *figure 6.15*.

When the reflected pulse travels back along the cord, it will travel through the incoming pulse; the resulting motion, formed by adding together the two pulses, may give a standing wave. A **standing wave** or stationary wave is one where the maximum displacement at a given point along the vibrating system does not vary with time. This is what happens on a stringed instrument, such as a guitar or violin, when the string is plucked or bowed.

### SAQ 6.4

The wave shown in *figure 6.16* travels down a piece of rubber cord at $10\,\mathrm{m\,s^{-1}}$. If the diagram represents time = 0, draw the state of the section of cord shown at the following times:

**a** 0.1s, **b** 0.25s, **c** 0.3s.

# Waves in a ripple tank

The behaviour of water waves can easily be seen in a ripple tank, and the reflection and refraction of these waves is shown in *figure 6.17*. One of the most important of these is *6.17d*, which shows the refraction of the waves as they pass from deep to shallow water. You can see that there is a change of wavelength. This change of wavelength is due to a change of speed in the shallow water.

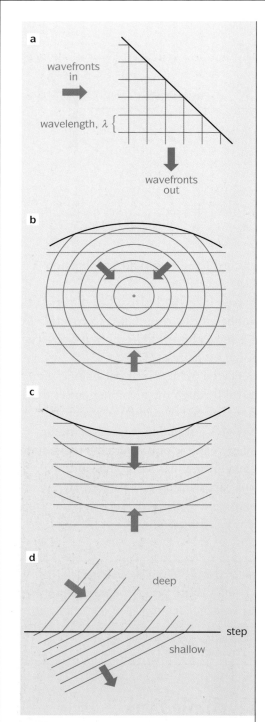

● **Figure 6.17** Waves in a ripple tank.

**a** Water waves reflected from a 45° barrier. Wavelength stays the same.

**b** Curved (concave) barrier. Reflected waves focus to a point.

**c** Curved (convex) barrier. Reflected waves fan out.

**d** Refraction at a 'step'. Wavelength shortens from deep to shallow.

When the waves pass from deep water to shallow water:

■ there is a decrease in wave speed and wavelength;

■ the frequency remains constant;

■ the ratio of the speed of the waves in deep water to that in shallow water is equal to that of their wavelengths.

### SAQ 6.5

What is the ratio of the wave speeds in deep and shallow water in **a** *figure 6.18a* and **b** *figure 6.18b*?

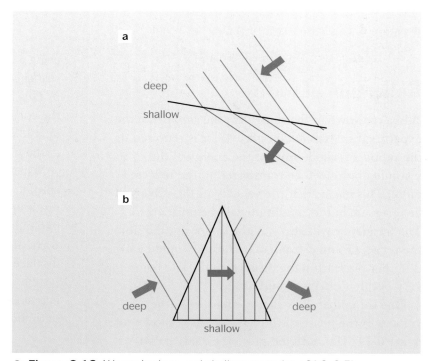

● **Figure 6.18** Waves in deep and shallow water (see SAQ 6.5).

## Investigating sound waves

The frequency, wavelength and amplitude of a sound wave can be very clearly shown using an oscilloscope and a microphone.

*Figure 6.19* shows the trace that you would get if a pure sine wave was fed to the microphone. If the time base of the oscilloscope was set at 0.5 ms per cm and the Y gain at 5 mV per cm, the frequency shown would be 870 Hz and the amplitude of the signal from the microphone would be 10 mV. (The grid is marked in 1 cm squares.)

### SAQ 6.6

Draw an oscilloscope screen grid like that in *figure 6.19*. Draw a wave with a frequency of 1000 Hz and an amplitude of 15 mV, and draw a wave that has half the amplitude and twice the frequency.

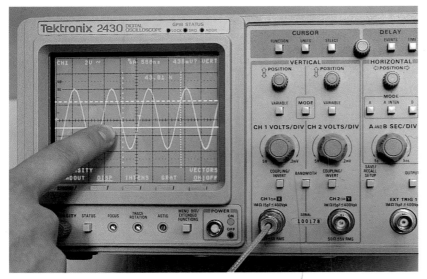

● *Figure 6.19* A pure sine wave as displayed on an oscilloscope screen.

## Experiment to measure the speed of sound in air

Two microphones are set up in front of a loudspeaker and their outputs are connected to the two inputs of a double-beam oscilloscope *(figure 6.20a)*. The traces on the screen show how the air is moving directly in front of each microphone. When the microphones are at the same distance from the loudspeaker, the traces shown in *figure 6.20b* are obtained. The sound waves have travelled the same distance to each microphone. One of the microphones is then moved back a distance *d* and the traces are now those in *figure 6.20c*. Knowing the time base speed of the oscilloscope (divisions per millisecond), you can find the time (*t*) taken for the sound to move the distance *d*. The speed of sound waves in air (*v*) is then given by

$$v = d/t$$

If you have access to a storage oscilloscope, the experiment can be done simply by using it as an accurate clock to measure the time for a sound pulse to travel down the laboratory and back.

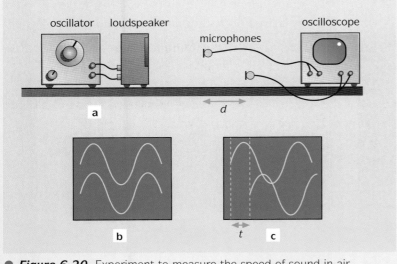

● *Figure 6.20* Experiment to measure the speed of sound in air.

## The quality of sound

There are many ways of making a sound; for example, screaming, playing a cello, singing, banging a tin sheet and humming. Some of these are pleasant and some unpleasant, and an oscilloscope trace may give some idea why. What is the difference between a noise and music? This is rather a difficult question to answer, especially since some people prefer Stravinsky to Beethoven or Vivaldi to Heavy Metal *(figure 6.21)*.

The waves that we have looked at before have been sine waves, and the oscilloscope can be used to show what this means. The oscilloscope describes the shape of the sound waves – and this property is known as their **quality** or timbre.

● *Figure 6.21* The difference between pleasant and unpleasant sounds depends on personal preference. In physics, the terms 'timbre' and 'noise' are used to describe specific properties of sound waves.

*Figure 6.22a* shows three wave forms; they all have the same frequency, so the pitch will be the same, but they have different shapes. The sine wave will sound a smooth tone, the sawtooth wave will be harsher and the square wave harsher still.

The oscilloscope shows us that, to a physicist, noise is a mixture of many different frequencies. **White noise** is sound that contains a large number of frequencies in a particular range *(figure 6.22b)*. White noise sounds like a hiss, the pitch depending on the frequency range. It can be an annoying background to weak radio signals.

You can use a microphone and oscilloscope to investigate the shape of the wave form for a series of different instruments, including the human voice. Investigate one note played on all the instruments, and then a range of notes played on just one of them. If possible, use a data logging device (or storage oscilloscope) to record the wave shape.

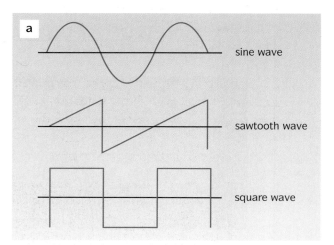

a — sine wave

sawtooth wave

square wave

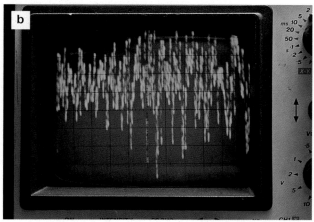

b

● *Figure 6.22* **a** Sine, sawtooth and square wave forms, and **b** white noise.

# Polarisation

Tie one end of a rubber rope to a post, get hold of the other end and pull the rope taut. If you flick your wrist, a loop forms in the rope and travels along it. This travelling loop or 'pulse' is an example of a 'quantum' (plural quanta) of wave energy; you can see that the loop looks very like a piece of a sine wave. If you send a series of pulses along the rope, you will see that, although each successive pulse may be sent in a different plane, each pulse only vibrates in one direction. This is exactly the same as a source of light. Light consists of quanta of waves with very high frequencies between $3 \times 10^{14}$ Hz and $1 \times 10^{15}$ Hz (compare this with the frequency range of FM radio – between 80 and 100 megahertz ($8 \times 10^7$ and $1 \times 10^8$ Hz)).

## SAQ 6.7

Light travels at a speed of $299\,792\,458\,\mathrm{m\,s^{-1}}$, a quantity that is often referred to by the symbol $c$. If we now use $c = 3 \times 10^8\,\mathrm{m\,s^{-1}}$, to what range of wavelengths does the range of frequencies just given correspond?

Each quantum emitted has vibrations in one plane but, because you receive many millions of quanta per second from a light source, it appears that the wave is vibrating in all directions.

A wave in which the plane of vibration is constantly changing is called an **unpolarised wave**. However, if the vibrations of a transverse wave are in one plane only, then the wave is said to be **plane polarised** (longitudinal waves cannot be polarised because they vibrate only along the direction of motion of the wave) *(figure 6.23)*.

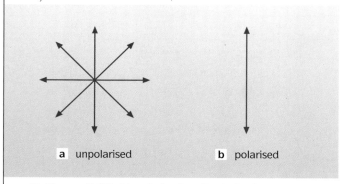

a unpolarised       b polarised

● *Figure 6.23* Unpolarised and polarised waves.

● *Figure 6.24* A hook as seen through a polarising filter. The different shades of colour represent different sizes of force.

Polarisation is easily observed with the rubber rope experiment described above, but it can also be shown with electromagnetic waves such as light, microwaves, radio and TV, the last one simply by rotating a set-top aerial and watching the effect on the picture.

Some examples of effects of polarisation with light are:

■ *Sunglasses*
These reduce glare by selecting one polarisation of light waves only, so the amount of un-polarised light reaching the eyes is reduced.

■ *Stresses in materials*
When materials are stressed (for instance, when they are used to hold something heavy together, e.g. a bridge), the surface distorts by very small amounts. If light reflected from the surface is viewed through a Polaroid, the bends in the surface can be seen as light and dark bands, because the different angles of reflection give different polarisations *(figure 6.24)*.

■ *Liquid-crystal displays*
Liquid-crystal displays on a calculator are usually polarised. You can investigate this effect by putting a piece of Polaroid over the display and rotating it.

A good simulation of the polarisation of scattered light in the atmosphere is to fill a transparent rectangular plastic tank with water and add a little milk to it (a few millilitres per litre should be sufficient). Shine a bright beam of light through the mixture, and observe the polarisation at different points around the tank using a piece of Polaroid and an LDR (light-dependent resistor) connected to a meter.

You can measure the amount of light transmitted through a pair of sunglasses when the lenses are placed over each other and rotated. See how the polarising material in the lenses *(figure 6.25)* reduces the quantity of light passing through.

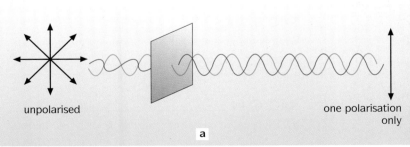

● *Figure 6.25* **a** Polaroid allows light to pass through it in one plane of polarisation only. **b** This effect can be used in photography, to reduce the amount of unpolarised light present in reflections.

# Reflection of light

Much of the work on reflection will have been covered in your GCSE course and so only a summary is given here, but with a few extensions.

## *Plane mirrors*

The reflection of light from a plane mirror *(figure 6.26)* can be summarised by the following laws:

- The angle of incidence (*i*) is equal to the angle of reflection (*r*).
- The incident ray, reflected ray and the normal to the surface at the point of incidence all lie in the same plane.

## *Images*

A **real image** is one through which the light rays actually pass and which can be formed on a screen. A **virtual image** is one through which the rays do not pass; they only appear to come from it. For an object, the image produced by a plane mirror is virtual and the same distance behind the mirror as the object is in front of it *(figure 6.27)*.

### SAQ 6.8

A plane mirror is fixed to the suspension of a moving-coil galvanometer that has a sensitivity of 5° per μA. If a current of 0.8 μA is passed through the meter, what is the movement of the light beam on a scale 3 m from the mirror?

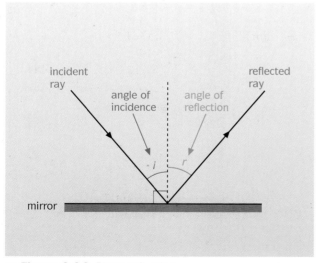

● **Figure 6.26** Plane reflection.

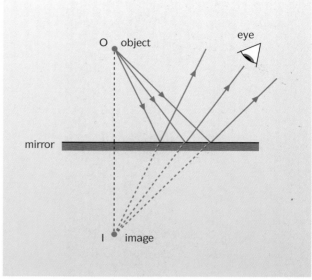

● **Figure 6.27** The position of an image seen in a plane mirror.

## *Uses of plane mirrors*

Among the many uses of plane mirrors are the following:

- kaleidoscope;
- overhead projector;
- to help direct light into the viewfinder in a single-lens reflex camera;
- the flat mirror in a Newtonian reflecting telescope;
- dental mirror.

### SAQ 6.9

A ray of light hits a plane mirror at an angle of incidence (*A*) and the mirror is then rotated through an angle $\theta$. Prove that the reflected ray will be rotated through an angle of $2\theta$.

### SAQ 6.10

What is the minimum length of plane mirror in which a man 1.8 m tall can see his full length?

### SAQ 6.11

a Discuss the problems of using back-silvered mirrors instead of front-silvered ones in a reflecting telescope.

b Why don't back-silvered mirrors present problems in everyday life?

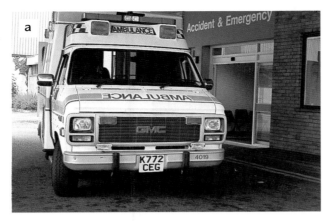

● *Figure 6.28* The emergency services make use of the fact that the 'backwards' writing can be read clearly in a rear-view mirror.

## SAQ 6.12

Draw an accurate diagram to show how the writing on the ambulance in *figure 6.28* appears to be the correct way round when viewed in the rear-view mirror of a car.

# Refraction of light

When light waves pass from air into a more dense medium such as water, glass or plastic they slow down while their frequency remains constant. The ratio of their speed in air (or more correctly in free space) to their speed in the medium is called the **refractive index** of the medium.

$$\text{refractive index} = \frac{\text{speed in free space}}{\text{speed in the medium}}$$

$$n = \frac{c}{c_m}$$

*Table 6.2* shows the refractive indices of some common substances (*figure 6.29*).

● *Figure 6.29* Diamonds sparkle partly because of their high refractive index. The shape to which they are cut is also very important.

The refractive indices in *table 6.2* are known as the *absolute* refractive indices of the materials, i.e. they are measured relative to the refractive index of a vacuum (1.00).

If light passes from one medium of absolute refractive index $n_1$ to another of absolute refractive index $n_2$, then the refractive index of the interface is written as $_1n_2$.

$$_1n_2 = \frac{n_2}{n_1} \qquad _1n_2 = \frac{1}{_2n_1}$$

| Material | Refractive index |
|---|---|
| Diamond | 2.42 |
| Ruby | 1.76 |
| Glass (flint) | 1.53–1.96 |
| Glass (crown) | 1.48–1.61 (refractive index of glass often taken as 1.5) |
| Glycerol | 1.47 |
| Magnesium fluoride* | 1.38 |
| Water | 1.33 |
| Ice | 1.31 |
| Air at STP† | 1.000 298 (often taken as 1.00) |

* Magnesium fluoride is used in non-reflective coatings (blooming of lenses).
† STP = standard temperature (298 K) and pressure ($10^5 \text{N m}^{-2}$).

● *Table 6.2* Refractive indices of some materials

## Waves and refraction

The change of speed when light moves from one medium to another gives a change of direction when the beam hits the boundary at an angle. When the light travels from a less dense medium such as air into a more dense medium such as glass, it bends towards the normal, bending away from the normal when its direction is reversed. The best way to understand this is by thinking about water waves. When they move up a sloping beach they slow down *(figure 6.30a)*, and when they meet it at an angle one side slows down before the other, and so the wave crests tend to become more parallel to the shore as they move inwards *(figure 6.30b)*.

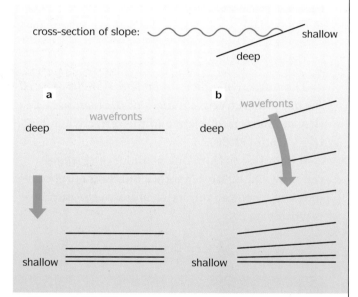

● **Figure 6.30** Water waves on a sloping beach, showing refraction.

Consider *figure 6.31a*. As the wave train meets the boundary, there will be $f$ crests per second meeting it, and so there must be $f$ crests per second leaving it. There can be no *build-up* of waves at the surface because there is no energy build-up. This means that the frequency of a wave is unchanged as it crosses from one medium to another.

If $c_1$ and $c_2$ are the wave speeds in mediums 1 and 2,

$$n = \frac{c_1}{c_2} \quad \text{and} \quad c = f\lambda \quad \text{and} \quad f \text{ is constant,}$$

$$n = \frac{c_1}{c_2} = \frac{\lambda_1}{\lambda_2}$$

Using *figure 6.31b*, consider triangles YAB and XAB. Since $n = \lambda_1/\lambda_2$ we have:

$$n = \frac{\lambda_1}{\lambda_2} = \frac{AB \sin(i)}{AB \sin(r)} = \frac{\sin(i)}{\sin(r)}$$

This law relating the angle of incidence ($i$), the angle of refraction ($r$) and the refractive index ($n$) was discovered in 1621 by Willebrod Snell, and is therefore known as **Snell's law**.

## Real and apparent depth

One other result of refraction is that pools of water look shallower (apparent depth) than they really are (real depth). It can be shown that the refractive index of the water (or indeed a pool of any liquid) is given by the formula:

$$\text{refractive index} = \frac{\text{real depth}}{\text{apparent depth}}$$

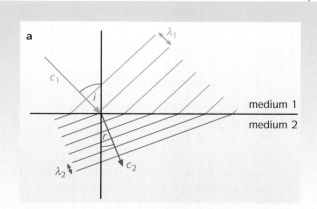

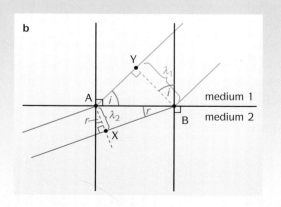

● **Figure 6.31** Wave refraction: wavelength changes but frequency does not.

## SAQ 6.13

Copy and complete the following table, using the refractive indices given in *table 6.2* where appropriate. (Assume that each material has the same refractive index for all wavelengths.)

| Material | Angle of incidence, $i$/degrees | Angle of refraction, $r$/degrees | Speed in material, $c_m$/m s$^{-1}$ | Wavelength in air, $\lambda$/nm | Wavelength in material, $\lambda_m$/nm |
|---|---|---|---|---|---|
| Water | 30 | | | 600 | |
| Ice | | 25 | | 450 | |
| Glycerol | | 30 | | 600 | |
| Glass ($n = 1.5$) | | 38 | | | 433 |
| Diamond | 50 | | | 600 | |

## SAQ 6.14

**a** Use the value 1.33 for the refractive index of water to draw an accurate scale diagram to show the position of the image of a fish 2 m below the surface of a pond when viewed from the point P above the water *(figure 6.32)*.

**b** Does this position agree with the formula that

$$\text{refractive index} = \frac{\text{real depth}}{\text{apparent depth}}?$$

**c** How does this position change when the observer's eye is moved further to the right along the line AP?

## SAQ 6.15

Is an object invisible if it has the same refractive index as the fluid it is in? Would this be a way of making an invisible man?!

## *Critical angle*

When light passes from a medium (such as glass, water or plastic) into a less dense medium (such as air) there is an angle of incidence where the angle of refraction is 90°. This angle of incidence in the more dense medium corresponding to an angle of refraction of 90° is called the **critical angle** (C) for that interface *(figure 6.33)*.

Considering the formula:

$$_2n_1 = \frac{\sin(i)}{\sin(r)} = \frac{\sin(C)}{\sin(90°)} = \sin(C)$$

therefore

$$_1n_2 = \frac{1}{_2n_1} = \frac{1}{\sin(C)}$$

For a water/air boundary, $_1n_2 = 1.33$, and this gives a critical angle of 48.5°. For a glass/air boundary with $_1n_2 = 1.5$, it is 42°.

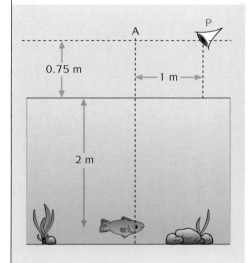

● *Figure 6.32*

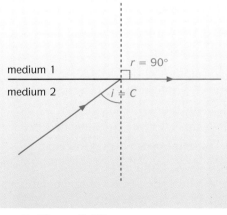

● *Figure 6.33*

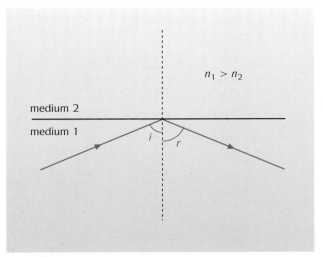

● *Figure 6.34* Total internal reflection.

## SAQ 6.16

What are the critical angles for the interfaces between the following materials and air: **a** ruby, **b** diamond and **c** glycerol? (Use the values from *table 6.2*.)

## SAQ 6.17

Prove that light cannot pass across the corner of a right-angled block of glass with a refractive index $n = 1.5$.

## Total internal reflection

If the angle of incidence in the more dense medium is increased past the critical angle, all the light is reflected back. This is known as **total internal reflection**, and the reflected ray obeys the normal laws of reflection (*figure 6.34*).

Total internal reflection explains why the surface of a swimming pool looks shiny when viewed from underneath, why you cannot see into an air-filled watch face under water and how prismatic binoculars work (*figure 6.35*). Mirages are caused by continuous internal reflection in differing air densities, and rainbows are caused by partial internal reflection in water droplets.

To demonstrate total internal reflection, put a layer of sugar solution in the bottom of a rectangular tank and then very carefully fill the rest of the tank with water taking care to mix the

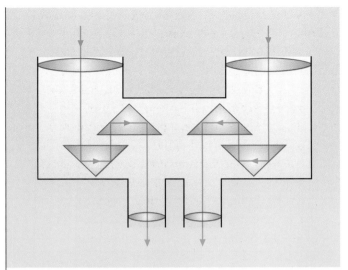

● *Figure 6.35* In prismatic binoculars, two 90° prisms set at 180° to each other are used to reduce the length of the instrument. This is achieved through total internal reflection in the prisms.

sugar as little as possible. Shine a beam of light into one end of the tank, upwards towards the water surface (*figure 6.36*). Describe and explain what you observe.

## Fibre optics

The transmission of light through a glass fibre is one of the most important applications of total internal reflection and is known as **fibre optics**. These glass fibres have a core a few micrometres ($10^{-6}$ m) in diameter and are covered with a layer

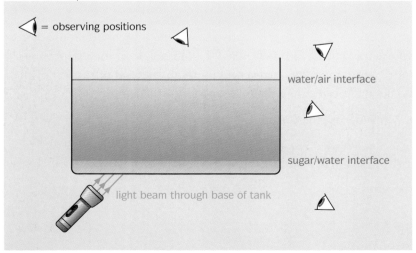

● *Figure 6.36* This apparatus can be used to demonstrate total internal reflection.

of glass cladding. The refractive indices of the core and the cladding are different. This means that when a light beam travels down the fibre, total internal reflection occurs at the interface between the core and the cladding, as long as the angle of incidence is large enough. At least a hundred of these fibres are sheathed in a polyurethane jacket to make a fibre optic cable *(figure 6.37)*.

For long-distance transmission, the light sources used are laser diodes, operating at a wavelength of 1310 nm, while simple light-emitting diodes (LEDs) are fine for short distances. Pulses of light can be used as a signal to carry information.

Fibre optic cables have a number of advantages – they are small, have a low mass, are quite flexible and can carry far more information than a conventional copper cable. For example, because light has such a high frequency ($10^{14}$–$10^{15}$ Hz), a single fibre optic cable can transmit up to half a million telephone conversations simultaneously!

The following list shows some of the uses of fibre optics:

- to see inside the human body, for endoscopy, inspection and keyhole surgery *(figure 6.38)*;
- for lighting road signs or models;
- in security fences;
- for telephone calls and cable TV.

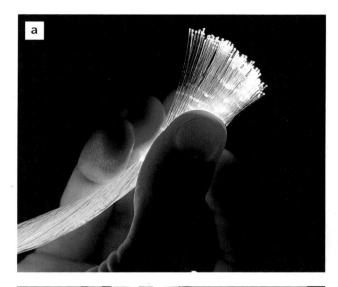

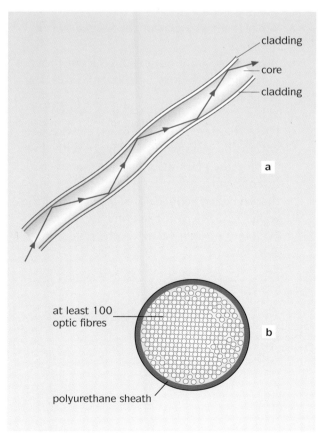

● *Figure 6.37*
**a** The path of a light beam in thin optical fibre.
**b** Cross-section through a fibre optic cable.

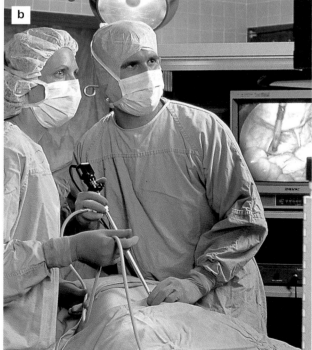

● *Figure 6.38*
**a** A bundle of optical fibres.
**b** Fibre optics are used in endoscopes, for internal surgery.

# SUMMARY

- A vibration or oscillation is a wobble. Any vibration can produce some kind of wave motion. A wave carries energy.

- There are two types of wave – longitudinal and transverse. Longitudinal waves have vibrations along the wave direction, whereas transverse waves have vibrations across the wave direction. Surface water waves, waves on a string and light waves are transverse. Sound and waves in the body of a tank of water consist of longitudinal waves.

- Wave speed = frequency × wavelength.

- When a wave is reflected from a fixed boundary there is a phase change of 180°.

- Transverse waves can be polarised.

- The frequency of sound waves can be measured using a cathode ray oscilloscope.

- The laws of reflection are:
  **a** angle of incidence = angle of reflection;
  **b** the object, the point of reflection and the image all lie in the same plane.

- Snell's law of refraction is: for an angle of incidence *i* and an angle of refraction *r*, the refractive index

  $$n = \frac{\sin (i)}{\sin (r)}.$$

- The critical angle *C* is the angle of incidence for which the angle of refraction is 90°:

  $$\sin (C) = \frac{1}{\text{refractive index}}.$$

- For angles of incidence above the critical angle, total internal reflection occurs.

- A very important application of total internal reflection is in fibre optics.

## *Questions*

1 If three plane mirrors are placed together so as to form the three sides of a right-angled corner *(figure 6.39)*, then any ray of light directed at any angle will be reflected back out of the corner. Prove that this is true.

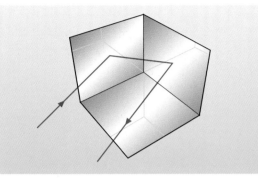

● *Figure 6.39*

2 A single glass fibre is bent into a perfect semicircle *(figure 6.40)*. The refractive index of the glass is 1.5.
  **a** What is the velocity of the light waves in the glass?
  **b** What is the minimum radius (*R*) of the outer surface before light escapes into the air at B?
  **c** What is the frequency of the light?
  **d** Draw diagrams to show how the waves within the glass would compare with those outside the glass when viewed on an oscilloscope with two traces. You may assume that the glass reduces the amplitude of the waves to 85% of those entering it. (Velocity of light in air can be taken as $3 \times 10^8 \, \text{m s}^{-1}$.)

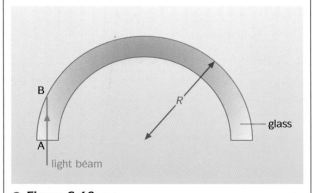

● *Figure 6.40*

# Electricity

● **Figure 7.1** We depend on electric currents and the properties of electric circuits to provide lighting in the dark. This city is Hong Kong.

## Electric current

Many people think that, when you switch on an electric light *(figure 7.1)*, the electric current surges out from the switch and along the wire – this is not true!

Electricity is already in a wire in the form of electrically charged particles – it simply requires energy to make it flow. This energy can come from a variety of sources – chemical reactions in an electric cell, rotation in a dynamo, light on a photoelectric cell, heat in a thermocouple, sound in a microphone, or mechanical stress in a piezo-electric crystal. When the charged particles flow, electrical energy is converted to other forms and appears as heat, chemical change, magnetism and so on.

But what is electricity? Consider a piece of metal wire – a very much enlarged view of which is shown in *figure 7.2*. The wire is composed of millions of atoms, each one with its cloud of electrons (see chapter 8). Although a sample of metal may be electrically neutral, it contains many electrons not held around particular nuclei, but free to wander through the metal (in a copper wire there are some $11 \times 10^{28}$ of these electrons per cubic metre). When these free electrons are made to move in a certain direction, we have an electric

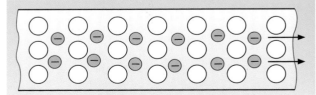

● **Figure 7.2** Atoms in a wire. Electric charge flows around them.

current. This can be done simply by connecting an electric cell or a battery between the two ends of the wire *(figure 7.3)*.

For a current to flow, a circuit has to be formed. One way of making current flow is to put a cell in the circuit. A cell is a device containing chemicals that react together to release electrical energy. A battery consists of several cells joined together. If the direction of the current is marked on the circuit diagram, it is shown going from the positive side of the cell, through the circuit to the negative side of the cell.

## SAQ 7.1

Why might a good electrical conductor also be a good conductor of heat?

## *The unit of electric charge*

Each electron carries only a very small amount of electric charge, and it is more convenient to use a larger unit when measuring practical units of charge. This unit is the **coulomb** (C). The much smaller charge $e$ is $1.6 \times 10^{-19}$ C. The charge on one electron is $-e$. You would need nearly $10^{19}$ electrons to have a charge of one coulomb!

The electrical charge passing any one point in a circuit in one second is called the **electric current**, and it is measured in amperes, A. Although the ampere is defined rigorously in chapter 1, it can also be expressed in the following way: a current of one ampere is flowing in a circuit if a charge of

one coulomb passes any point in that circuit in one second. That is,

$$\text{current, } I/\text{A} = \frac{\text{charge passed, } Q/\text{C}}{\text{time taken, } t/\text{s}}$$

or

$$I = \frac{Q}{t} \quad \text{and} \quad Q = It$$

For example, we can calculate the current in a wire if a charge of 180 C passes a given point in 2 minutes. Then

$$\text{current} = \frac{Q}{t} = \frac{180}{120} = 1.5\,\text{A}$$

(NB time in seconds)

## SAQ 7.2

A current of 14 A flows for one hour. How much charge passes a point in the circuit?

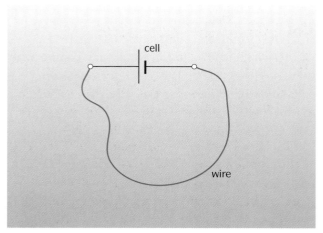

● **Figure 7.3** A cell causes current to flow around a circuit. An electric current is a flow of charged particles.

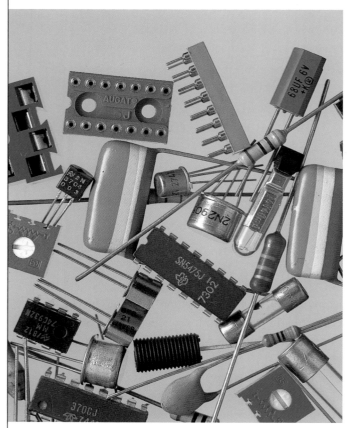

● **Figure 7.4** A selection of electrical components, including resistors, fuses, capacitors and microchips.

| Symbol | Component name | Symbol | Component name |
|---|---|---|---|
|  •——————• | connecting lead |  | variable resistor |
| 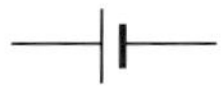 —⊣⊢— | cell |  | microphone |
| 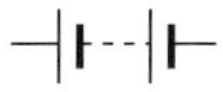 —⊣⊢··⊣⊢— | battery of cells | 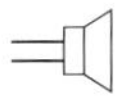 | loudspeaker |
| 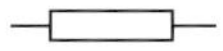 —▭— | resistor |  | fuse |
|  —o o— | power supply | 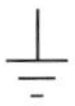 | earth |
|  —•— | junction of conductors |  —Ⓧ— | alternating signal |
| 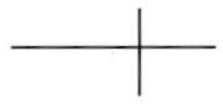 —┼— | crossing conductors (no connection) |  —⊣⊢— | capacitor |
| 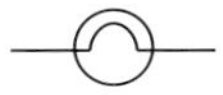 —Ⓧ— | filament lamp |  | inductor |
| 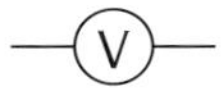 —Ⓥ— | voltmeter | 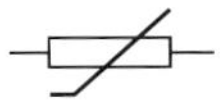 | thermistor |
|  —Ⓐ— | ammeter | 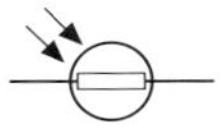 | light-dependent resistor (LDR) |
|  —o o— | switch (or make contact) | 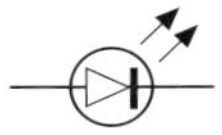 | light-emitting diode (LED) |

● *Figure 7.5* Names of electrical objects and their circuit symbols.

## Electrical symbols

There is a variety of electrical components *(figure 7.4)*. You should be able to recognise the symbols for the components in *figure 7.5* and be able to use them in a variety of circuits.

## Conservation of charge

When a current flows round the simple circuit shown in *figure 7.6a*, the current at any point in the circuit is the same wherever it is measured – no electrons are lost from the circuit. This important principle of physics is called the **conservation of charge**. One implication of this is that a circuit must be formed for a current to flow; the electrons cannot 'fall out' of the end of the wire.

The production of heat and light by an electric current is due to the electrons converting energy to other forms as they move round the circuit. You can compare this with runners in a steeplechase; they 'lose' most of their energy over the jumps in the same way that electrons transfer energy when passing through a bulb or resistor *(figure 7.6b)*. (We assume that the runners do not lose any energy on the flat!)

## Potential, and potential difference

The electrical potential energy of a unit positive charge (that is, +1 coulomb) at a point in the circuit is called the **potential** at that point.

The variation in potential round a number of simple circuits is shown in *figure 7.7*. You can see that there is a large change in potential where there is a large transformation of energy. We assume a steady but very small loss of usable energy in the connecting leads and usually ignore it completely (see SAQ 7.18).

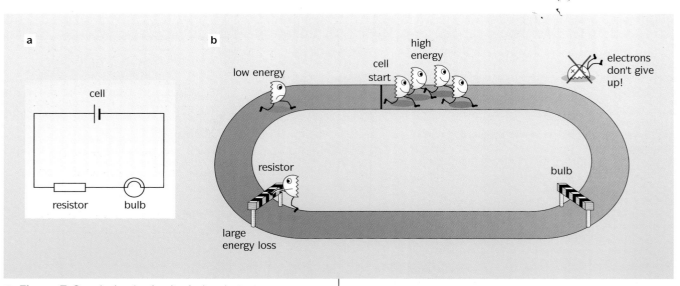

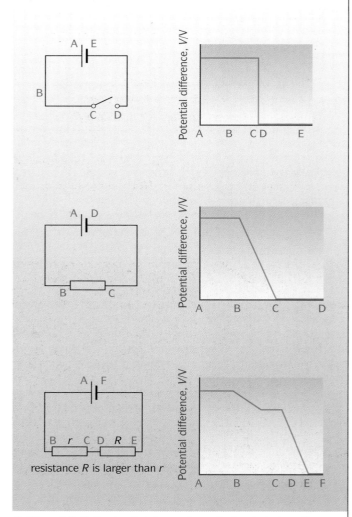

● **Figure 7.6** **a** A simple circuit. **b** An electron 'steeplechase'.

● **Figure 7.7** Some circuits, and graphs to show how the potential changes around them.

The difference in electrical potential energy between any two points in the circuit is shown by the potential difference (or voltage) between them. The **potential difference** (p.d.) between two points in a circuit is defined as the work done in moving a unit positive charge from one point to the other.

$$\text{potential difference} = \frac{\text{energy (work done)}}{\text{charge}}$$

$$V = \frac{W}{Q}$$

The units for potential difference are therefore joules per coulomb, usually referred to as **volts**: $1\,\text{volt (V)} = 1\,\text{joule/coulomb}\;(J\,C^{-1})$.

Notice that, when no charge flows, there can be no change of potential and therefore no potential difference between two parts of a circuit that are connected.

## *Electrical power*

Power is the rate at which work is done or energy is transferred:

$$\text{power} = \frac{\text{energy (work done)}}{\text{time}}$$

and so

$$\text{electrical power} = \frac{\text{potential difference} \times \text{charge}}{\text{time}}$$

But current = charge/time and therefore

$$\text{power/W} = (\text{p.d./V}) \times (\text{current/A})$$

## SAQ 7.3

Calculate how much electrical energy is supplied by a 12 V battery when:

**a** a charge of 2400 C passes through it;

**b** a current of 2.5 A flows from it for 15 s.

## SAQ 7.4

A 12 V car battery supplies 200 A for 2 s to the starter motor *(figure 7.8)*. How much energy is drawn from the battery?

## Resistance

When a cell is connected across a piece of metal, a potential difference is formed across it. This makes the free electrons move through it, colliding with each other and the atoms of the metal as they do so. These collisions restrict the movement of the electrons, and this property is called the **resistance** of the metal *(figure 7.9)*. If the metal is heated, the collisions become more violent, and the resistance of the metal therefore increases.

The resistance of a piece of material is related to the current flowing through it and the potential difference between its ends by the equation:

$$\text{resistance} = \frac{\text{potential difference}}{\text{current}}$$

$$R = \frac{V}{I}$$

The units of resistance are **ohms** ($\Omega$) and a specimen has a resistance of one ohm (1 $\Omega$) if a current of 1 A flows through it when there is

● *Figure 7.8* A car battery has to supply large amounts of current to operate the starter motor in the engine.

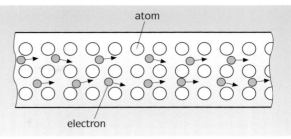

● *Figure 7.9* Electrons 'bouncing off' atoms is a simplified representation of how resistance occurs.

a p.d. of 1 V between its ends. An insulator is a material of very high resistance *(figure 7.10)*.

## SAQ 7.5

Calculate the current through the following resistors:
**a** 120 $\Omega$ connected to 240 V; **b** 4700 $\Omega$ connected to 12 V; **c** 10 k$\Omega$ connected to 6 V; **d** 2.5 M$\Omega$ connected to 25 V.

## SAQ 7.6

What is the resistance of the following:
**a** a lamp that draws 2 A from a 12 V supply;
**b** a kettle that draws 4 A from a 240 V supply?

## Further notes on electrical power

Since power = *VI*, and *V* = *IR* for a resistance, we can write

$$\text{power} = VI = I^2R = \frac{V^2}{R}$$

● *Figure 7.10* An insulator has a very high resistance. If the potential difference across it is high enough, the insulator may 'break down', and allow high currents to flow.

It is very important to remember that *V* is the potential difference across the resistor and *I* is the current flowing through the resistor. The significance is shown in the following example.

Suppose that a power station produces a current of 100 A at a potential of 200 kV. It feeds the electricity into power lines 15 km long, with a resistance per unit length of $0.2\,\Omega\,km^{-1}$. What is the power produced by the station? What is the power dissipated as heat in the power lines?

For the first part we can use $P = VI$. So

$$P = 200 \times 10^3 \times 100 = 20\,MW$$

Notice that the question only gives the potential produced by the station and *not* the potential difference across the lines. To calculate the power loss in the lines we must use $P = I^2R$. So

$$P = 100^2 \times 3 = 30\,kW$$

This is much less than that produced by the station.

### SAQ 7.7

What power is supplied to the heater of an electric bar fire with a resistance of $50\,\Omega$ connected to the mains 240 V supply?

### SAQ 7.8

What is the power loss down a copper connecting lead 50 cm long with a resistance of $0.005\,\Omega\,m^{-1}$ when it carries a current of 1.5 A?

● **Figure 7.11**  A power station and electrical transmission lines. What is the power loss across these lines (see SAQ 7.9)?

### SAQ 7.9

The electrical transmission cable from a power station is 25 km long and carries a current of 100 A *(figure 7.11)*. The resistance per kilometre of the cable is $0.2\,\Omega$ and the potential at the power station end of the cable is 400 kV. What is the power loss in the cable?

# Series and parallel circuits

## *Series circuits*

In the circuit shown in *figure 7.12* the current is the same at all points round the circuit. Such a circuit is called a **series circuit**. No electrons are lost in the circuit, and so the number per second passing any point must be the same as that passing any other point. The electrons transfer energy to the surroundings as they flow round, most energy being transferred in components such as lamps and resistors. Very little energy is transferred in the connecting leads. The total potential difference is $V = V_1 + V_2$.

## *Parallel or branched circuits*

If there is a branch in the circuit with two or more components (light bulbs, for example) in parallel *(figure 7.13a)*, then the potential difference between the two ends of the branch is the same no matter across which bulb you measure it, i.e. $V_1 = V_2$. (Lights in a house are wired like this.) Compare this with a tall building with two staircases *(figure 7.13b)* – it does not matter which staircase you

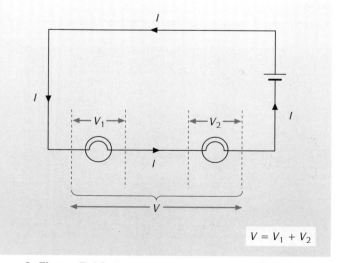

$$V = V_1 + V_2$$

● **Figure 7.12**  An example of a series circuit.

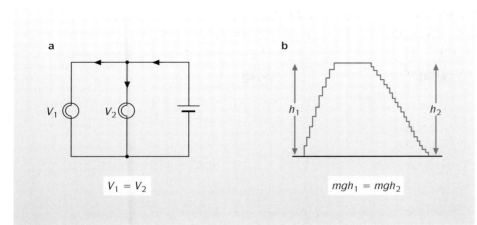

$V_1 = V_2$

$mgh_1 = mgh_2$

● **Figure 7.13** **a** An example of a parallel circuit.
**b** See text.

come down by, you will still have reduced the gravitational potential energy by the same amount.

If the supply voltage is constant, the current in one branch of the circuit has no effect on the current in the other. You may be able to understand this by thinking of a bath with water running out of one plug hole *(figure 7.14)* and into a tank below. A pump, connected to the tank, constantly refills the bath to keep the water level constant. Making another hole in the bottom of the bath will not affect the amount or speed of the water running from the first plug hole – only the total water flow is changed. The pump has to work harder to maintain the level in the bath.

## SAQ 7.10

You have five 1.5 V cells. How would you connect all five of them to give a potential of: **a** 7.5 V, **b** 1.5 V, **c** 4.5 V?

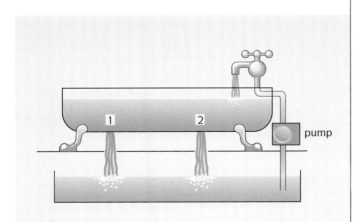

● **Figure 7.14**

## Ammeters and voltmeters

Because of what they measure, ammeters and voltmeters are connected differently *(figure 7.15)*. Ammeters are always connected in series, since they measure the current flowing through a circuit. For this reason, an ammeter should have as low a resistance as possible (less than an ohm) so that as little energy as possible is transferred in the ammeter itself.

However, voltmeters measure the difference in potential between two points on the circuit. For this reason, they are connected in parallel, and they should have a very high resistance (1 MΩ = $10^6\,\Omega$ or more is ideal), so as to take as little current as possible. (A voltmeter with a resistance

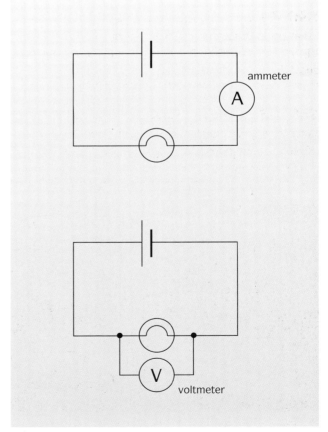

ammeter

A

V

voltmeter

● **Figure 7.15** How to connect up an ammeter and a voltmeter.

of 10 MΩ measuring a p.d. of 2.5 V will take a current of $2.5 \times 10^{-7}$ A and draw 0.625 μJ of energy from the circuit every second.)

Some measuring instruments are shown in *figure 7.16*.

## Kirchhoff's first law

Consider the branched circuit in *figure 7.17*. The electrons have a choice of branch, but using the idea of conservation of charge you can see that the number going into the junction per second must equal the number leaving it. In other words, 'what goes in must come out'.

This idea is expressed formally as: the currents at a junction are conserved. This is known as **Kirchhoff's first law** and is important for making calculations involving branched circuits.

## Series and parallel resistors

Resistors are rarely found singly in circuits, so we will now consider series and parallel resistors (*figure 7.18*).

In the series circuit (*figure 7.18a*) the current ($I$) flowing through $R_1$ and $R_2$ is the same, and so the potential differences across them are

$$V_1 = IR_1 \qquad \text{and} \qquad V_2 = IR_2$$

The effective resistance of the two resistors is given by the formula:

$$R = R_1 + R_2$$

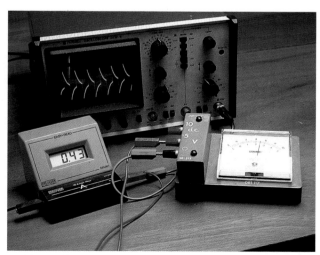

● **Figure 7.16** Electrical measuring instruments.

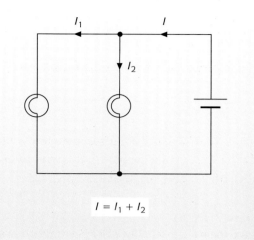

$$I = I_1 + I_2$$

● **Figure 7.17** The example of a parallel circuit, illustrating Kirchhoff's first law.

For three resistors in series this becomes:

$$R = R_1 + R_2 + R_3$$

In the circuit in *figure 7.18b* we have two resistors in parallel. The effective resistance ($R$) of the two resistors $R_1$ and $R_2$ connected in parallel is given by the following equation:

$$\frac{1}{R} = \frac{1}{R_1} + \frac{1}{R_2}$$

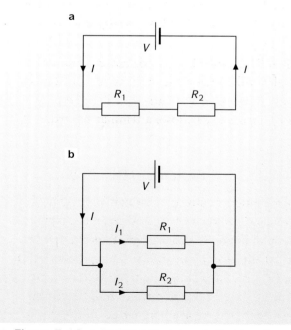

● **Figure 7.18 a** Resistors in series. **b** Resistors in parallel.

This can also be written as

$$R = \frac{R_1 R_2}{R_1 + R_2}$$

For three resistors in parallel the formula is:

$$\frac{1}{R} = \frac{1}{R_1} + \frac{1}{R_2} + \frac{1}{R_3}$$

Notice that two, or more, resistors in parallel always have a smaller resistance than the same number of resistors connected in series.

### SAQ 7.11

Calculate the resistance of the following combinations: **a** $100\,\Omega$ and $200\,\Omega$ in series; **b** $100\,\Omega$ and $200\,\Omega$ in parallel; **c** $100\,\Omega$ and $200\,\Omega$ in series and this in parallel with $200\,\Omega$.

### SAQ 7.12

Calculate the current flowing through the following when a p.d. of $12\,V$ is applied across the ends: **a** a resistance of $500\,\Omega$; **b** $500\,\Omega$ and $1000\,\Omega$ in series; **c** $500\,\Omega$ and $1000\,\Omega$ in parallel.

### SAQ 7.13

You are given one $200\,\Omega$ resistor and two $100\,\Omega$ resistors. What total resistances can you obtain by connecting some, none, or all of these resistors in various combinations?

Generally, connecting two or more resistors in parallel will increase the current drawn from a supply (remember the bath with the two plug holes). *Figure 7.19* shows a familiar hazard.

## Ohm's law and temperature

The variation of current through a metallic conductor can be investigated using the circuit shown in *figure 7.20a*. We can show the results graphically as in *figure 7.20b*. The gradient of the line ($V/I$) is constant and equal to the resistance ($R$) of the conductor. If the ratio of p.d. to current remains constant for a number of different p.d. values (as it does in the graph here), the material is said to be an ohmic conductor.

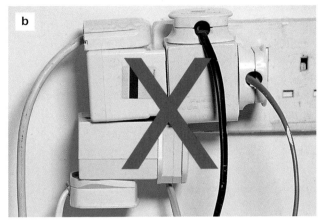

● *Figure 7.19* **a** Correct and **b** incorrect use of an electrical adapter. In **b**, too many appliances (resistances) are connected in parallel. This reduces the total resistance and increases the current drawn, to the point where it becomes dangerous.

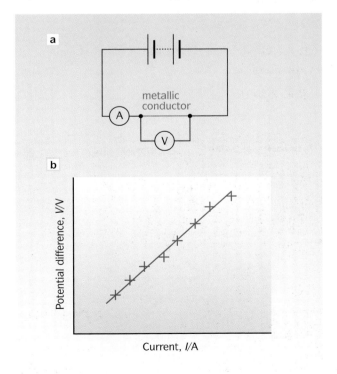

● *Figure 7.20* The current through a metallic conductor.

**Ohm's law** states that the ratio of p.d. to current is a constant for metals at a constant temperature. This means that we can work out the resistance of a specimen at a given temperature if we know the current through it and the p.d. across it. However, if we change the p.d. across it and the current through it, we can only *predict* how it will behave if it obeys Ohm's law.

But what if the temperature is not constant?

## Resistance and temperature change

If the temperature of the wire changes, then its resistance will also change. In a solid, for example a wire, the atoms 'wobble' about their fixed positions. If the wire is heated, the electrons make more violent and frequent collisions with the atoms of the metal, because the higher temperature makes the atoms 'wobble' more. For this reason, the resistance of the wire increases.

## The filament lamp

When a current is passed through a fine metal wire, such as that in a filament in a lamp *(figure 7.21)*, changes take place. The current produces a heating effect, which in turn leads to an increase in

● *Figure 7.21* The metal filament in a light bulb produces both light and heat.

the filament's resistance. This change is about a factor of ten from when the lamp is off (and cold) to when it is operating (and hot – some 1750 °C).

A graph of the variation of current with voltage for a filament lamp is shown in *figure 7.22*. The temperature of the lamp at each point is also shown.

### SAQ 7.14

a Use the graph in *figure 7.22* to find the resistance of the lamp at temperature intervals of 150 °C from 100 °C to 1000 °C.

b Use your values to plot a resistance–temperature graph for the lamp. What does this tell you?

## The thermistor

This is a device that is primarily used because of its large change in resistance with temperature. Thermistors are made from metal oxides such as those of manganese and nickel. There are two distinct types of thermistor:

■ The resistance of one type decreases approximately exponentially with increasing temperature (these are called negative temperature coefficient thermistors). Ones commonly used in school may have a resistance of a few tens of ohms at 100 °C, rising to many thousands of ohms at room temperature.

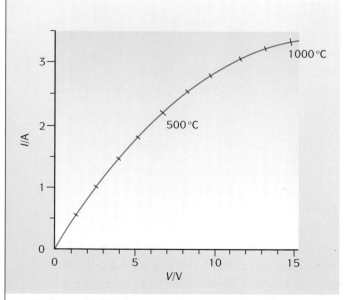

● *Figure 7.22* Current–voltage curve for a filament lamp.

The resistance of the other type rises abruptly at a definite temperature, usually around 100–150°C (these are called positive temperature coefficient thermistors).

The change in their resistance with temperature gives thermistors many uses:

■ Water temperature sensors in cars and ice sensors on aircraft wings – if ice builds up on the wings, the thermistor senses this temperature drop and a heater is activated, removing the ice.

■ Baby alarms – the baby rests on an air-filled pad, and as he breathes, air from the pad passes over a thermistor, keeping it cool; if the baby stops breathing, the air movement stops, the thermistor warms up and an alarm sounds.

■ Fire sensors – the rise in temperature activates an alarm.

■ Overload protection in razor sockets – if the razor overheats, the thermistor's resistance rises rapidly and cuts off the circuit.

## SAQ 7.15

The two graphs in *figure 7.23* show the resistance of a specimen of metal wire at two different temperatures, $\theta_1$ and $\theta_2$.

**a** Calculate the resistance of the wire at each temperature.

**b** Which graph shows the higher temperature, $\theta_1$ or $\theta_2$?

## SAQ 7.16

The graph in *figure 7.24* was obtained by measuring the resistance of a particular thermistor as its temperature changed.

**a** What is its resistance at (i) 20°C and (ii) 45°C?

**b** At what temperature is its resistance (i) 5000 $\Omega$ and (ii) 2000 $\Omega$?

**c** What is its rate of change in resistance with temperature at (i) 20°C, (ii) 45°C, and (iii) 70°C?

## *Resistivity*

The resistance of a piece of material depends not only on the material itself but also on its dimensions. You can use conducting putty to find out how the resistance of a given volume of such putty depends on its length and its cross-sectional area.

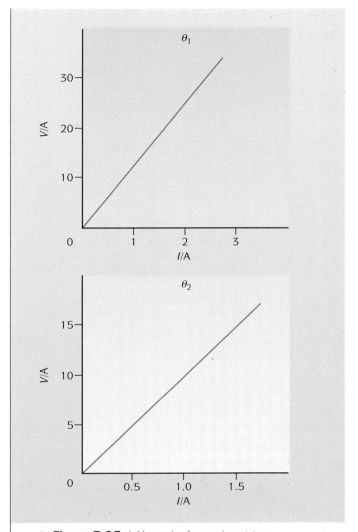

● **Figure 7.23** *I–V* graphs for a wire at two temperatures, $\theta_1$ and $\theta_2$ (see SAQ 7.15).

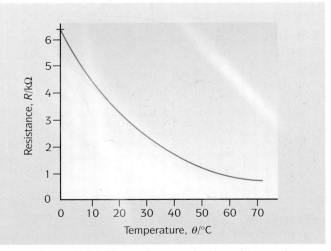

● **Figure 7.24** The resistance of a thermistor as the temperature changes (see SAQ 7.16).

You should find that the resistance of a sample depends on:

■ length – the longer the specimen, the higher the resistance;
■ cross-sectional area – the smaller the cross-sectional area, the higher the resistance.

| Material | Resistivity/($\Omega$m) | Material | Resistivity/($\Omega$m) |
|---|---|---|---|
| Silver | $1.60 \times 10^{-8}$ | Eureka‡ | $49.0 \times 10^{-8}$ |
| Copper | $1.69 \times 10^{-8}$ | Carbon | $35\text{–}5000 \times 10^{-8}$ |
| Nichrome* | $1.30 \times 10^{-8}$ | Germanium | $0.65$ |
| Aluminium | $3.21 \times 10^{-8}$ | Silicon | $2.3 \times 10^{3}$ |
| Lead | $20.8 \times 10^{-8}$ | Pyrex glass | $10^{12}$ |
| Manganin † | $44.0 \times 10^{-8}$ | PTFE** | $10^{13}\text{–}10^{16}$ |
| Mercury | $69.0 \times 10^{-8}$ | Quartz | $5 \times 10^{16}$ |
| Graphite | $800 \times 10^{-8}$ | | |

It is therefore useful to define the resistance of the material in general rather than for a particular shaped specimen. For this reason, a property known as the **resistivity** $\rho$ (Greek *rho*) of the material is used. It is defined as the resistance of a specimen of the material with unit length and unit cross-sectional area.

$$\text{resistivity} = \frac{\text{resistance} \times \text{area}}{\text{length}}$$

$$\rho = \frac{RA}{L}$$

Resistivity is measured in ohm metres ($\Omega$m). The higher the resistivity of a material, the greater will be the resistance of a specimen of a given shape and size. *Table 7.1* gives the resistivities of some well known materials.

You cannot quote values for the resistivities of solutions generally, because these depend upon their concentrations and temperatures, but for example the resistivity of pure water is $2.5 \times 10^{5}\,\Omega$m and that of a saturated solution of sodium chloride is $0.04\,\Omega$m at $20\,°C$.

We shall now work through an example. The resistance of a piece of eureka in the form of a thin wire of cross-sectional area $2.5 \times 10^{-7}\,m^2$ is $5.0\,\Omega$ when measured between its ends. What is the length of the wire? Using the above formula

$$\text{length} = \frac{\text{resistance} \times \text{area}}{\text{resistivity}} = \frac{5.0 \times 2.5 \times 10^{-7}}{49.0 \times 10^{-8}}$$

$$= 2.6\,m$$

Silver has one of the lowest resistivities, followed by copper. In spite of this, it is aluminium that is used for overhead power cables, primarily because of its low density and also its relatively low cost compared with silver.

\* Nichrome – an alloy of nickel, copper and aluminium used in electric fires because it does not oxidise at $1000\,°C$.
† Manganin – an alloy of 84% copper, 12% manganese and 4% nickel.
‡ Eureka (constantan) – an alloy of 60% copper and 40% nickel.
\** Poly(tetrafluoroethene) or Teflon.

● **Table 7.1** Resistivities of various materials

The reciprocal of resistivity is known as the **conductivity** and is measured in $\Omega^{-1}\text{m}^{-1}$:

$$\text{conductivity} = \frac{\text{length}}{\text{resistance} \times \text{area}} = \frac{L}{RA}$$

The resistance of any conducting material depends on the following factors:

■ the material itself;
■ its length;
■ its cross-sectional area;
■ its temperature.

### SAQ 7.17
Calculate the lengths of 0.5 mm diameter manganin wire needed to make resistance coils with resistances of:
**a** $1\,\Omega$, **b** $5\,\Omega$, **c** $10\,\Omega$. (Use the resistivity values quoted in *table 7.1*.)

### SAQ 7.18
Calculate the resistance of $1\,cm^3$ of copper when in the form of:

**a** a wire of cross-sectional area $4 \times 10^{-7}\,m^2$ (between the ends);

**b** a thin sheet 0.5 mm thick (between the faces of the sheet).

## SAQ 7.19

When a wire is stretched, it gets a little thinner and so its resistance increases. This effect is used in a device called a strain gauge, used in engineering. Calculate the change in resistance of a copper wire of original cross-sectional area $1.2 \times 10^{-7} \, \text{m}^2$ in such a gauge when its length is increased from 1.00 cm to 1.05 cm.

## SAQ 7.20

A tube of mercury allows a current of 0.5 A to pass through it when connected to a battery of negligible resistance. What current will pass through it when it is poured into a beaker of half the radius of the original column?

# Questions

1  A certain 12 V car battery is labelled 48 ampere hour (Ah).
   a  What does 48 Ah mean?
   b  How much electrical energy does the battery contain?
   c  How long could it supply a continuous current of 200 A needed to start a car?
   d  What is the mean power supplied at a current of 40 A if the potential across its terminals remains constant?
   e  When current flows **from** a battery a current also flows **through** it. Use this information to explain why batteries get hot when supplying large currents.

2  This question refers to *figure 7.25* containing a negative temperature coefficient thermistor (T).
   Calculate:
   a  the resistance of each branch of the circuit;
   b  the current in each branch of the circuit;
   c  the total resistance of the four components;
   d  the potential difference between points A and B.
   What will happen to the potential difference between A and B if the thermistor is warmed?

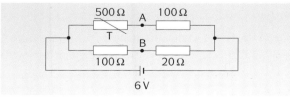

● **Figure 7.25**

# SUMMARY

■ An electric current is a flow of charged particles (usually electrons).

■ The coulomb (C) is the SI unit of charge, $Q$.

■ Current, $I$, is the rate of flow of charge: $Q = It$.

■ The potential difference between two points is a measure of the difference in the energy of the electrons at these points, and is defined as the work done in moving a unit positive charge (+1 C) from one point to the other.

■ Resistance, $R$, is defined by the equation

$$R = \frac{V}{I}.$$

So a resistance of $1 \, \Omega$ is present in a device if a current of 1 A flows in the device when there is a potential difference of 1 V across it.

■ Kirchhoff's first law states that the currents at a junction are conserved, or 'what goes in must come out'.

■ Two resistors connected in series have a greater total resistance than either of the two individual resistors. The formula for the total resistance, $R$, is

$$R = R_1 + R_2.$$

■ Two resistors connected in parallel have a smaller total resistance than either of the two individual resistors. The formula for the total resistance, $R$, is

$$\frac{1}{R} = \frac{1}{R_1} + \frac{1}{R_2}.$$

■ As the temperature of a metal increases, so does its resistance.

■ Ohm's law states that the ratio of potential difference to current is constant for a metal at a constant temperature.

■ A thermistor is a device that exhibits a rapid change in resistance at a particular temperature.

■ The resistivity, $\rho$, of a material is defined as

$$\rho = \frac{RA}{L},$$

where $R$ is the resistance of a sample of the material, $A$ is its cross-sectional area and $L$ is its length.

■ The work done, $W$, in moving a charge $Q$ across a potential difference $V$ is given by $W = QV$.

■ Electrical power, $P = VI$. The power dissipated in a resistor is given by $P = I^2R$.

## Chapter eight

# Atomic structure

## By the end of this chapter you should be able to:

1 demonstrate a qualitative understanding of the α-particle scattering experiment and the evidence that it provides for the existence of and the small size of the nucleus;

2 describe a simple model for the nuclear atom to include protons, neutrons and orbital electrons;

3 distinguish between nucleon number (mass number) and proton number (atomic number);

4 understand that an element can exist in various isotopic forms each with a different number of neutrons;

5 use the conventional notation for the representation of nuclides.

● *Figure 8.1* J. J. Thomson at work.

## Looking inside the atom — is there a central nucleus?

The idea that matter was composed of very small particles called **atoms** was first suggested by the Greeks some two thousand years ago. However, it was not until the middle of the nineteenth century that any ideas about the *inside* of the atom were proposed.

It was the English scientist J. J. Thomson *(figure 8.1)* who suggested that the atom was a neutral particle made of a positive charge with lumps of negative charge (electrons) in it. At the time he was also investigating the nature of the particles in cathode rays (produced when an electrically charged plate is heated) and he presented his conclusions at the Royal Institution on 30 April 1897. He could not measure the charge and mass of the cathode ray particles separately, but it was clear that a new particle, probably much smaller than the hydrogen atom, had been discovered. Thomson called this particle a 'corpuscle' and used this term for many years even after the name **electron** had been given to it by most other physicists. Since atoms are neutral and physicists had

already discovered a negatively charged part of an atom, it meant that there were both positive and negative charges in an atom. We now call this the **plum pudding model** of the atom (positive pudding with negative plums!).

Other experiments show that the electron has a mass of $9.11 \times 10^{-31}$ kg ($m_e$) and a charge of $-1.6 \times 10^{-19}$ C ($-e$).

## Rutherford scattering and the nucleus

Early in the twentieth century, many physicists were investigating the recently discovered phenomenon of radioactivity, the process whereby atoms emit radiation. One kind of radiation they found consisted of what they called α-particles (*alpha-particles*). These α-particles were known to be smaller than atoms, and had relatively high energies, and therefore they were useful in experiments designed to discover what atoms were made of.

In 1906 while experimenting with the passage of α-particles through a thin mica sheet, Rutherford *(figure 8.2)* noticed that most of the α-particles passed straight through. In 1911 he carried out a further series of experiments with Geiger and

Marsden at the University of Manchester using gold foil in place of the mica. They fired α-particles at a piece of gold foil only $10^{-6}$ m thick. Most of the α-particles went straight through, some were deflected slightly but about 1 in 20 000 were deflected through an angle of more than 90°, so that they appeared to bounce back off the foil. When Geiger told Rutherford of the results, Rutherford wrote: 'It was quite the most incredible event that has happened to me in my life. It was almost as incredible as if you fired a 15 inch shell at a piece of tissue paper and it came back and hit you.' This gave Rutherford the idea that atoms might be mostly empty space with a central **nucleus** that only affected the α-particles when they came close to it. A very simple analogy (or model) of the experiment is shown in *figure 8.3*.

When you roll a ball-bearing down a slope towards the 'cymbal', it can be deflected; but even if it is rolled directly at the cymbal's centre, it does not come back but rolls over it and carries on to the other side. However, using the 'tin hat' shape,

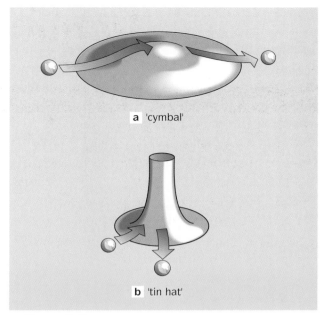

a 'cymbal'

b 'tin hat'

● *Figure 8.3*

with a much narrower but higher central bulge, any ball-bearings rolled close to the centre will be markedly deflected, and those rolled directly towards it will come straight back. The shape of the cymbal represents the shape of the electric field of an atom in the 'plum pudding' model: low central intensity and spread out. The 'tin hat' represents that for the nuclear model: high central intensity and concentrated.

The paths of an α-particle near a nucleus are shown in *figure 8.4*. Rutherford reasoned that the large deflection of the α-particle must be due to a very small positively charged nucleus with a very

● *Figure 8.2* Ernest Rutherford (on the right) in the Cavendish Laboratory, Cambridge, England. He had a loud voice that could disturb sensitive apparatus and so the notice was a joke aimed at him.

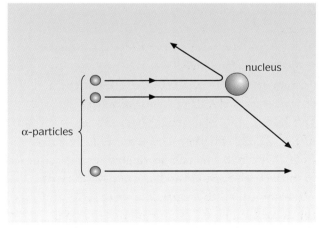

nucleus

α-particles

● *Figure 8.4* Possible paths of an α-particle near a nucleus.

large electric field near its surface. From his experiments he calculated that the diameter of the gold nucleus was about $10^{-14}$m. The very large deflection of the α-particle is due to the electrostatic repulsion between the positive charges of the α-particle and the positive charges in the nucleus of the atom. The closer the path of the α-particle gets to the nucleus, the greater will be this repulsion.

## SAQ 8.1

Rutherford's scattering experiments were done in an evacuated container. Why was this necessary?

# The structure of the nucleus

The nucleus is small and positively charged, but what is it made up of? After Rutherford had described the size and mass of the nucleus, scientists carried out experiments to see what it was made from. They discovered two kinds of particles.

## Discovery of the proton

The first subnuclear particle to be identified was the proton, discovered by Rutherford in 1919. He used the apparatus shown in *figure 8.5*. Alpha-particles were passed through some nitrogen gas in a cylinder and flashes of light were seen on a screen. Rutherford knew that these flashes were produced by the impact of particles on the screen. A sheet of aluminium foil in front of the screen prevented any α-particles reaching it, so there must have

been some other kind of particle emitted by the foil when the α-particles hit the foil. Measurements were made of the deflection of the penetrating particles that passed between the foil and the screen, and these measurements proved that they were particles smaller than most nuclei and with a positive charge equal in size to that of the electron. These particles were called **protons**.

## Discovery of the neutron

Rutherford had shown that nuclei contained positively charged protons, and then in 1932 Chadwick discovered the neutron. This was an electrically neutral particle with a slightly greater mass than the proton. He did this by bombarding beryllium with α-particles emitted from polonium *(figure 8.6)*. A penetrating neutral radiation was produced by the beryllium, and when this radiation fell on a

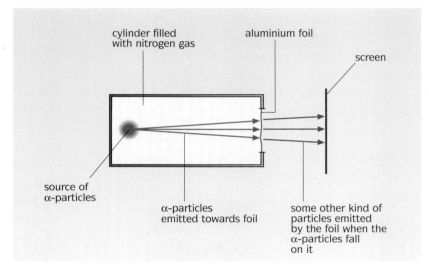

● *Figure 8.5* A schematic diagram of the apparatus used to discover the proton.

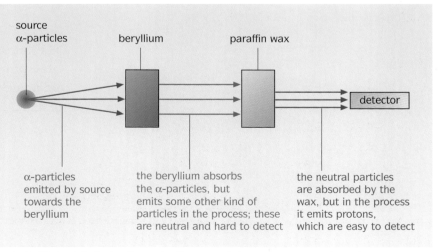

● *Figure 8.6* A schematic diagram of the apparatus used to discover the neutron.

piece of paraffin wax, protons with high energy were emitted by the paraffin. The neutral radiation was difficult to detect, but the protons emitted as a result of this neutral radiation were quite easily detected. The conclusion was that the penetrating neutral radiation consisted of uncharged particles that could pass easily through matter without a large transfer of energy, since particles with no charge produce virtually no ionisation of matter. Chadwick called these particles **neutrons**. Neutrons collide elastically with atoms, transferring more energy to a light atom than to a heavy one. For this reason, neutron radiation is especially damaging to human tissue.

## SAQ 8.2

Explain carefully why neutron radiation is so dangerous to humans.

## *A simple atom model*

We have discussed protons and neutrons in the atom, but what about the electrons? They orbit the nucleus in a cloud, some closer to and some further from the centre of the nucleus. This fact and the experiments and discoveries covered in this chapter so far suggest a model for the atom like the one shown in *figure 8.7*. From this model it looks as though all matter, including ourselves, is mostly empty space. For example, if we scaled up the hydrogen atom so that the nucleus was the size of a 1 cm diameter marble, the orbiting electron would be a grain of sand some 800 m away!

# Nucleons and electrons

We will start this section with a summary of the particles mentioned so far (*table 8.1*). All nuclei, except the lightest form of hydrogen, contain protons and neutrons and each nucleus is described by the number of protons and neutrons that it contains. Protons and neutrons in a nucleus are collectively

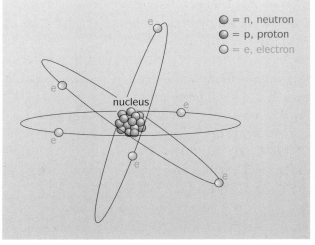

● *Figure 8.7* A simple model of the atom.

called **nucleons**. For example, in a nucleus of gold, there are 79 protons and 118 neutrons, giving a total of 197 nucleons altogether. The total number of nucleons in a nucleus is called the **nucleon number** (mass number) $A$. This is equal to the sum of the number of neutrons in the nucleus, **neutron number** $N$, and the number of protons, **proton number** (atomic number) $Z$, i.e. $A = N + Z$.

Any nucleus can be represented by the symbol for the element with the nucleon number and proton number as shown below:

$$\text{nucleon number} \atop \text{proton number} \quad \text{element symbol} \qquad {}^{A}_{Z}X$$

oxygen ${}^{16}_{8}O$    gold ${}^{197}_{79}Au$    uranium ${}^{235}_{92}U$

A specific combination of protons and neutrons in a nucleus is called a **nuclide.**

The proton and nucleon numbers of some common elements are shown in *table 8.2*.

| Particle | Nature | Relative mass (proton = 1)* | Charge† |
|----------|--------|------------------------------|---------|
| proton | proton | 1 | $+e$ |
| neutron | neutron | 1 | 0 |
| electron | electron | 0.0005 | $-e$ |
| alpha ($\alpha$) | helium nucleus ‡ | 4 | $+2e$ |

\* The numbers given for the masses are approximate.

† $e = 1.6 \times 10^{-19}$ C.

‡ Notice that the $\alpha$-particle is in fact a helium nucleus. It contains two protons and two neutrons.

● *Table 8.1* Summary of particles that we have met so far in this chapter

| Element | Nucleon number | Proton number | Element | Nucleon number | Proton number |
|---|---|---|---|---|---|
| hydrogen | 1 | 1 | bromine | 79 | 35 |
| helium | 4 | 2 | silver | 107 | 47 |
| lithium | 7 | 3 | tin | 120 | 50 |
| beryllium | 9 | 4 | iodine | 130 | 53 |
| boron | 11 | 5 | caesium | 133 | 55 |
| carbon | 12 | 6 | barium | 138 | 56 |
| nitrogen | 14 | 7 | tungsten | 184 | 74 |
| oxygen | 16 | 8 | platinum | 195 | 78 |
| neon | 20 | 10 | gold | 197 | 79 |
| sodium | 23 | 11 | mercury | 202 | 80 |
| magnesium | 24 | 12 | lead | 206 | 82 |
| aluminium | 27 | 13 | bismuth | 209 | 83 |
| chlorine | 35 | 17 | radium | 226 | 88 |
| calcium | 40 | 20 | uranium | 238 | 92 |
| iron | 56 | 26 | plutonium | 239 | 94 |
| nickel | 58 | 28 | americium | 241 | 95 |

● **Table 8.2** Proton and nucleon numbers of some nuclides

## SAQ 8.3

How many neutrons are in the following nuclei shown in *table 8.2*: **a** nitrogen, **b** bromine, **c** silver, **d** gold and **e** mercury?

You can see from *table 8.2* that, as the nuclei get heavier, so the ratio of the number of neutrons to the number of protons gets larger. For example, for light elements such as hydrogen, helium, carbon and oxygen, the ratio is 1, for iron it is 1.15

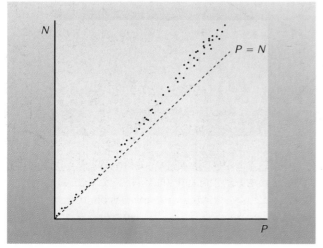

● **Figure 8.8** A graph of neutron number $N$ against proton number $P$ for the naturally occurring elements.

and for uranium it has risen to 1.59. After this it starts to fall again for the artificial elements with $Z > 92$. A graph of neutron number against proton number for the naturally occurring elements is shown in *figure 8.8*.

## SAQ 8.4

What charges have the following, in terms of $e$:
**a** proton, **b** neutron, **c** nucleus, **d** molecule, **e** α-particle?

# Size of the nucleus

We now know that the nucleus is composed of two different sorts of particle (protons and neutrons). Since Rutherford's experiments, it has been proved that a good estimate of the radius ($r$) of a nucleus of nucleon number $A$ is given by:

$$r = r_0 A^{1/3}$$

where $r_0$ is a constant equal to $1.2 \times 10^{-15}$ m.

For example, the gold nucleus (nucleon number 197) would have an approximate radius of

$$r = 1.2 \times 10^{-15} \times 197^{1/3} = 6.98 \times 10^{-15} \text{ m}$$

A useful unit when measuring distances of this size is the femtometre (fm) (sometimes called the fermi); 1 femtometre = 1 fm = $10^{-15}$ m. The radius of the gold nucleus in the example above is therefore 6.98 fm.

# Isotopes and their uses

Although atoms of the same element may be identical chemically, their nuclei may be slightly different. The number of protons in the nucleus of an atom determines what element it is; helium always has 2 protons, carbon 6, oxygen 8, neon 10, radium 88, uranium 92 and so on.

However, the number of neutrons in a given element can vary. Take neon as an example. Three different naturally occurring forms of neon are:

$$^{20}_{10}\text{Ne} \qquad ^{21}_{10}\text{Ne} \qquad ^{22}_{10}\text{Ne}$$

The first has 10 neutrons in the nucleus, the second 11 and the third 12. These three types of neon are called **isotopes** of neon. Each isotope has the same number of protons (for neon this is 10) but a different number of neutrons. The word 'isotope' comes from the Greek *isotopos* (same place), because all isotopes of the same element have the same place in the Periodic Table of elements.

Any atom is electrically neutral (it has no net positive or negative charge), so the number of orbiting electrons must equal the number of protons in the nucleus of the atom. If an atom gains or loses an electron, it is no longer electrically neutral and is called an **ion**.

For an atom, the number of protons (and hence the number of orbiting electrons) determines the chemical properties of the atom. The number of protons and the number of neutrons determine the nuclear properties. It is important to realise that, since the numbers of protons, and therefore the number of electrons, in isotopes of the same element are identical, they will all have the same chemical properties but different nuclear properties.

Hydrogen has three important isotopes, $^1\text{H}$, $^2\text{H}$ (deuterium) and $^3\text{H}$ (tritium) *(figure 8.9)*. $^1\text{H}$ and deuterium occur naturally, but tritium has to be made. Deuterium and tritium form the fuel of many fusion research reactors. Hydrogen is the most abundant element in the Universe, because it consists of just one proton and one electron, and this is the simplest structure possible for an atom *(figure 8.10)*.

The relative atomic masses of isotopes will also be different. There are differences too in some of their physical properties, such as density and boiling point. For example, heavy water, water containing deuterium, has a boiling point of 104°C under normal atmospheric pressure.

*Table 8.3* gives details of some other common isotopes.

## SAQ 8.5

There are seven naturally occurring isotopes of mercury with nucleon numbers (relative abundances) of 196 (0.2%), 198 (10%), 199 (16.8%), 200 (23.1%), 201 (13.2%), 202 (29.8%) and 204 (6.9%).

**a** What are the proton and neutron numbers for each isotope?

**b** Suggest what the average relative atomic mass of naturally occurring mercury might be.

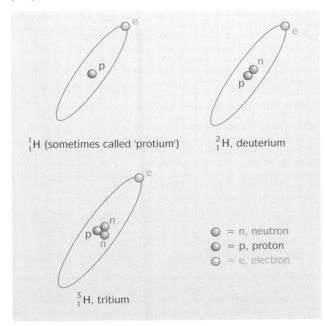

● *Figure 8.9* The isotopes of hydrogen.

● *Figure 8.10* The Horsehead Nebula in Orion. The large coloured regions are expanses of dust and gas, mostly hydrogen, that are ionised by nearby stars and emit light. The dark 'horse head' is where the areas of gas and dust remain in atomic form and block out the light from behind.

| Element | A | Z | N |
|---------|-----|-----|-----|
| hydrogen | 1 | 1 | 0 |
| hydrogen | 2 | 1 | 1 |
| carbon | 12 | 6 | 6 |
| carbon | 14 | 6 | 8 |
| oxygen | 16 | 8 | 8 |
| oxygen | 18 | 8 | 10 |
| neon | 20 | 10 | 10 |
| neon | 21 | 10 | 11 |
| potassium | 39 | 19 | 20 |
| potassium | 40 | 19 | 21 |
| strontium | 88 | 38 | 50 |
| strontium | 90 | 38 | 52 |
| caesium | 135 | 55 | 80 |
| caesium | 137 | 55 | 82 |
| lead | 206 | 82 | 124 |
| lead | 208 | 82 | 126 |
| radium | 226 | 88 | 138 |
| radium | 228 | 88 | 140 |
| uranium | 235 | 92 | 143 |
| uranium | 238 | 92 | 146 |

● **Table 8.3** Some common isotopes

## SAQ 8.6

Group the following into isotopes and name them using the Periodic Table:

| | A | B | C | D | E | F | G | H |
|---|----|----|----|----|----|----|----|----|
| Proton number | 20 | 23 | 21 | 22 | 20 | 22 | 22 | 23 |
| Nucleon number | 44 | 50 | 46 | 46 | 46 | 48 | 50 | 51 |

## SAQ 8.7

A nucleus of strontium has a nucleon number of 90 and a proton number of 38. Describe the structure of the strontium nucleus.

## SAQ 8.8

An element has several isotopes.

**a**  How do their nuclei differ?

**b**  In what ways are their nuclei the same?

## *Structure of the nucleus and the strong nuclear force*

As you know, there are two kinds of particle in the nucleus of an atom: protons, which carry a unit positive charge; and neutrons, which are uncharged (see page 80). It is therefore quite surprising that the nucleus holds together at all – you would expect the electrostatic repulsions from all those positively charged protons to blow it apart. The fact that this does not happen is very good evidence for the existence of another attractive force between the nucleons. This is called the **strong nuclear force**. It only acts over very short distances ($10^{-14}$m), and it is what holds the nucleus together.

In small nuclei the strong force from all the nucleons reaches most of the others in the nucleus, but as we go on adding protons and neutrons the balance becomes much finer. The longer-range electrostatic force affects the whole nucleus, but the short-range strong nuclear force of any particular nucleon only affects those nucleons around it – the rest of the nucleus is unaffected. In a large nucleus the nucleons are not held together so tightly, and this can make the nucleus unstable. However, the more protons there are in a nucleus, the greater the electric forces between them, and we need a few extra neutrons to help 'keep the protons apart'. This is why heavy nuclei have more neutrons than protons.

The variation of neutron number with proton number is shown in *figure 8.8*. You can see that for light elements these two numbers are the same, but they become very different for heavy elements. Adding more neutrons helps to keep the nucleus stable; but when the number of protons is greater than 83, adding more neutrons is not enough, and all elements with a proton number of greater than 83 are unstable.

Most atoms that make up our world are stable; that is, they do not change as time goes by, which is quite fortunate really! However, some are less stable and give out radiation. Whether or not an atom is unstable depends on the numbers of protons and neutrons in its nucleus. Hydrogen-1 (1p), helium-4 (2p,2n), carbon-12 (6p,6n) and oxygen-16 (8p,8n) are all stable – but add extra neutrons and the situation changes.

For example, add a neutron to helium-4 and you get helium-5, a very unstable nucleus. Carbon-14, with two neutrons more than the stable isotope carbon-12, is used in carbon dating. The radio-active isotope carbon-14 ($^{14}_{6}C$) is present in very small quantities in all natural substances containing carbon-12. The amount of carbon-14 present in living material, in a plant or animal, is kept constant, because the living 'thing' is continually taking in other materials containing carbon-14 (for example, in the things animals eat). When the plant or animal dies, the amount of carbon-14 reduces at a steady rate because it emits radiation. The quantity of carbon-14 in a substance can be measured quite accurately, and so the age of the substance can be determined *(figure 8.11)*.

## Uses of isotopes

- Archaeological and geological dating
- Medical – diagnostic and treatment
- Fluid flow tracking and measurement
- Sterilisation of foodstuffs
- Fertiliser tracers
- Nuclear pacemakers for the heart

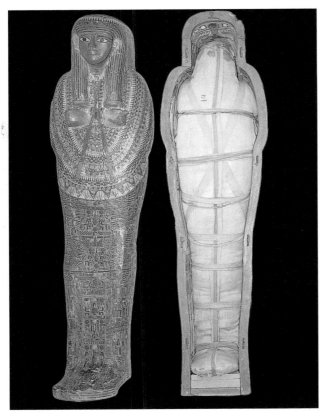

● *Figure 8.11*  Carbon dating is used to measure the ages of historical artefacts, such as this Egyptian mummy.

## SUMMARY

- The α-particle scattering experiment provides evidence for the existence of a small, positively charged nucleus at the centre of the atom. The atom consists of a small, relatively heavy central nucleus composed of protons (with a positive charge $+e$) and neutrons (with no charge). The nucleus is surrounded by a cloud of orbiting electrons (carrying a negative charge $-e$). An atom is an electrically neutral particle.

- The number of protons and neutrons in the nucleus of an atom is called its *nucleon number* ($A$).

- The number of protons in the nucleus of an atom is called its *proton number* ($Z$).

- The number of neutrons in the nucleus of an atom is called its *neutron number* ($N$).

- The nucleon number is the sum of the proton number and neutron number: $A = Z + N$.

- Isotopes are atoms of the same element (with the same proton number) but different neutron numbers.

- Different isotopes (or nuclides, if referring to the nucleus only) can be represented by the notation:

$$^{\text{nucleon number}}_{\text{proton number}}\text{element symbol}$$

## Question

1  If an α-particle of a given energy is fired directly at a nucleus, the repulsion between it and the nucleus will slow it down until it eventually comes to rest at a distance $r_0$ from the nucleus. This distance is 45 m for gold (proton number 79).

   a  If $r_0$ is directly proportional to the charge on the nucleus of the target atoms, work out the distances of closest approach for alpha particles of the same energy when fired directly at the nuclei of targets of (i) lead   (ii) iron   (iii) carbon (use *table 8.2* for the proton number). Comment on your answers.

   b  What difference would have been observed if Rutherford had performed the alpha scattering experiment using a similar thickness of aluminium foil?

# Answers to self-assessment questions

For help with checking, answers are sometimes given to one more significant figure than is justified by the data.

The value of $g$ that has been used throughout the working of these questions has been $9.8\,\mathrm{m\,s^{-2}}$.

## Chapter 1

1.1 **a** Equation balances.

    **b** Equation does not balance.

    **c** Equation balances.

1.2 Your estimates may vary by quite large amounts, but the right orders of magnitude are:

    **a** $1\,\mathrm{kg}$      **b** $500\,\mathrm{m^3}$      **c** $0.05\,\mathrm{m^3}$

    **d** $100\,\mathrm{N}$      **e** $300\,\mathrm{K}$      **f** $50\,\mathrm{Hz}$

1.3 See *figure*. From the formula, we can get $g = 4\pi^2\,L/T^2$. From the graph, $L/T^2 = 0.248\,\mathrm{m\,s^{-2}}$. So $g = 4\pi^2 \times 0.248\,\mathrm{m\,s^{-2}} = 9.79\,\mathrm{m\,s^{-2}}$. [You may not obtain exactly this value using your graph.]

1.4 Less violent motion, because the greater mass of the smoke particles slows them down and makes them less affected by collisions with air molecules.

1.5 **a** $5.0 \times 10^{25}$

    **b** $4.8 \times 10^{22}$

    **c** $4.0 \times 10^{-9}\,\mathrm{g}$

    **d** $2.6\,\mathrm{mg}$

1.6 **a** $1.59 \times 10^{-10}\,\mathrm{m}$

    **b** $3.41 \times 10^{-10}\,\mathrm{m}$

1.7 See *table right*.

1.8 See *figure*.

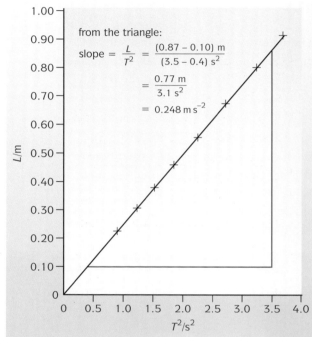

Graph of $T^2$ against $L$ for a single pendulum (SAQ 1.3)

from the triangle:

$$\text{slope} = \frac{L}{T^2} = \frac{(0.87 - 0.10)\ \mathrm{m}}{(3.5 - 0.4)\ \mathrm{s^2}}$$

$$= \frac{0.77\ \mathrm{m}}{3.1\ \mathrm{s^2}}$$

$$= 0.248\ \mathrm{m\,s^{-2}}$$

● **Answer for** SAQ 1.3

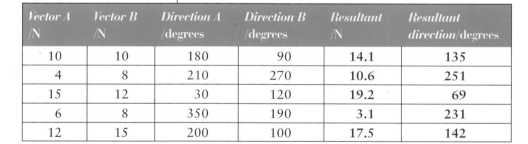

| Vector A /N | Vector B /N | Direction A /degrees | Direction B /degrees | Resultant /N | Resultant direction/degrees |
|---|---|---|---|---|---|
| 10 | 10 | 180 | 90 | 14.1 | 135 |
| 4 | 8 | 210 | 270 | 10.6 | 251 |
| 15 | 12 | 30 | 120 | 19.2 | 69 |
| 6 | 8 | 350 | 190 | 3.1 | 231 |
| 12 | 15 | 200 | 100 | 17.5 | 142 |

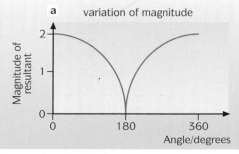

**a** variation of magnitude

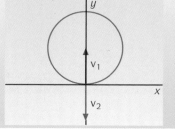

**b** including direction: locus of vector head

● **Answer for** SAQ 1.8

1.9    20.8 N, 59°

1.10  **a**  $x$, 17.3 N;  $y$, 10 N

  **b**  $x$, 1.7 m s$^{-1}$;  $y$, $-4.7$ m s$^{-1}$

  **c**  $x$, $-5.2$ m s$^{-2}$;  $y$, $-3$ m s$^{-2}$

  **d**  $x$, 77.3 N;  $y$, 20.7 N

1.11  **a**  100 N        **b**  489 N

## Chapter 2

2.1  **a**  The extra distance travelled during each second.

  **b**  10.2 m s$^{-1}$

  **c**  1.14 m s$^{-2}$, $-0.11$ m s$^{-2}$

  **d**  Reaction time to the gun at the start.

  **e**  See *figure*.

  **f**  200 m. Area under graph = distance covered by athlete.

2.2  100 m

2.3  Train stops. Distance travelled = 2500 m.

2.4  **a**  800 m      **b**  1.25 m s$^{-2}$, 750 m

  **c**  5.0 s      **d**  1000 m      **e**  90 m

2.5  40 m on the Earth, 99 m on the Moon.

2.7  6.4 m s$^{-1}$

## Chapter 3

3.1  470 N s

3.2  1.86 N s

3.3  33 000 N

3.4  15 m s$^{-2}$, 67.5 m

3.5  9900 N; either, for same stopping force, stopping distance increases to 49 m, or, for same stopping distance, force needs to increase to 12 200 N.

3.6  16 800 N

3.7  245 s

3.8  1770 N

## Chapter 4

4.1  $P = 338$ N, $N = 725$ N

4.2  67 N by gardener; 160 N by legs

4.3  173 g. By this method, weighing could be carried out with a limited selection of relatively small masses.

4.4  9.83 N

4.5  7800 N

4.6  761 N

## Chapter 5

5.1  1270 J

5.2  $7.1 \times 10^9$ J. This energy becomes increased internal energy of the air. The temperature of the air must rise.

5.3  10.1 J

5.4  2200 J; 9.9 m s$^{-1}$

5.5  Car: 28 000 N s, 490 000 J
     Van: 40 000 N s, 400 000 J

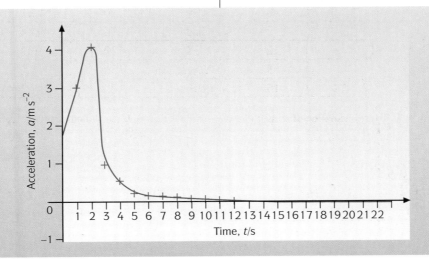

● *Answer for* SAQ 2.1e

5.6   0.983

5.7   0.983

5.8   2400 W

5.9   600 W

5.10 **a** 520 000 W

**b** 0.69. Rest of power is converted into heat and sound energy.

## Chapter 6

6.1   20.24 kHz

6.2   115 m s$^{-1}$

6.3

| Station | Wavelength, $\lambda$/m | Frequency, $f$/MHz |
|---|---|---|
| Radio 1 (FM) | **3.07** | 97.6 |
| Radio 2 (FM) | **3.33** | 90.2 |
| Radio 3 (FM) | **3.25** | 92.4 |
| Radio 4 (FM) | **3.17** | 94.6 |
| Radio 4 (LW) | 1500 | **0.20** |
| Radio 5 | 693 | **0.43** |

6.4   See *figure*.

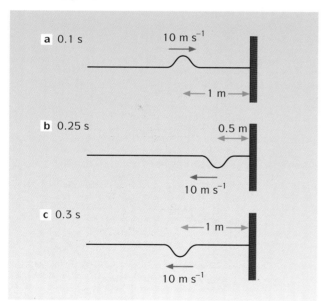

● *Answer for* SAQ 6.4

6.5   **a** 1.7 : 1   **b** 1.9 : 1

6.6   See *figure*.

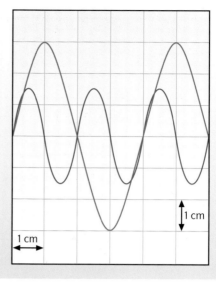

● *Answer for* SAQ 6.6

6.7   $10^{-6}$ m to $3 \times 10^{-7}$ m

6.8   42 cm

6.9   The angle of incidence increases by $\theta$, so the angle of reflection also increases by $\theta$, and therefore the total change (rotation) of the beam of light is $2\theta$.

6.10  0.9 m

6.11  **a** Multiple reflections from the front and back surfaces will blur the image.

**b** In everyday life, the object is close to the mirror and produces a large image, and we do not notice the multiple reflections. In telescopes, the object is very distant and produces a tiny image, and the multiple reflections are very noticeable.

6.12  See *figure*.

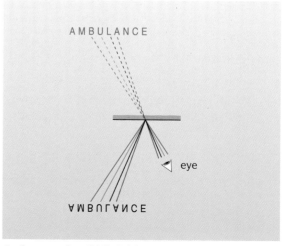

● *Answer for* SAQ 6.12

6.13

| Material | Angle of incidence, $i$/degrees | Angle of refraction, $r$/degrees | Speed in material, $c_m$/m s$^{-1}$ | Wavelength in air, $\lambda$/nm | Wavelength in material, $\lambda_m$/nm |
|---|---|---|---|---|---|
| Water | 30 | 22 | $2.3 \times 10^8$ | 600 | 450 |
| Ice | 34 | 25 | $2.3 \times 10^8$ | 450 | 340 |
| Glycerol | 47 | 30 | $2.0 \times 10^8$ | 600 | 410 |
| Glass ($n = 1.5$) | 67 | 38 | $2.0 \times 10^8$ | 650 | 433 |
| Diamond | 50 | 19 | $1.2 \times 10^8$ | 600 | 250 |

6.14 a See *figure*.

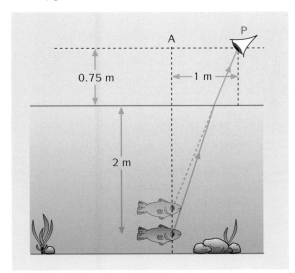

● **Answer for** SAQ 6.14a

b Yes.

c Moves further up and towards P.

6.15 Yes – but you would have to make sure there was no reflection. Also, although for the sake of simplicity in this book we say that refractive index is constant, in fact it varies with the frequency of the incident light.

6.16 a 34.6°    b 24.4°    c 42.9°

6.17 Hint: Construct a diagram and consider the critical angles; remember that there are two boundaries to consider, at 90° to one another.

## Chapter 7

7.1 There are many electrons free to carry the thermal or electrical energy.

7.2 50.4 kC

7.3 a 28.8 kJ        b 450 J

7.4 4800 J

7.5 a 2 A           b 2.6 mA

c 0.6 mA        d 10 μA

7.6 a 6 Ω           b 60 Ω

7.7 1152 W

7.8 5.6 mW

7.9 50 kW

7.10 a In series.     b In parallel.

c See *figure*.

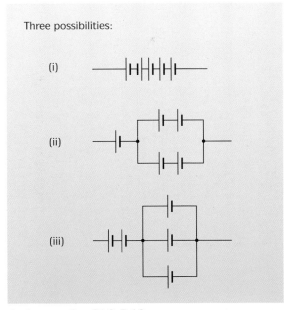

Three possibilities:

(i)

(ii)

(iii)

● **Answer for** SAQ 7.10c

7.11 a 300 Ω        b 67 Ω        c 120 Ω

7.12 **a** 24 mA **b** 8 mA **c** 36 mA

7.13 Total resistances possible are (in $\Omega$): 0, 40, 50, 67, 75, 100 (two ways), 167, 200, 250, 300 and 400.

7.14 **a** 100°C: 2.5 $\Omega$    700°C: 6.3 $\Omega$
    250°C: 3.3 $\Omega$    850°C: 11 $\Omega$
    400°C: 3.9 $\Omega$    1000°C: 22 $\Omega$
    550°C: 4.9 $\Omega$

   **b** See *figure*. Resistance increases almost linearly with temperature until around 600°C, where the filament resistance starts to increase much faster.

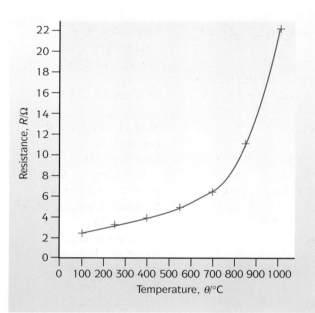

● *Answer for* SAQ 7.14b

7.15 **a** 12.5 $\Omega$, 10 $\Omega$    **b** $\theta_1$

7.16 **a** (i) 3.2 k$\Omega$    (ii) 1.6 k$\Omega$

   **b** (i) 10°C    (ii) 35°C

   **c** (i) $-0.1\,\Omega\,°C^{-1}$    (ii) $-0.05\,\Omega\,°C^{-1}$

   (iii) Almost $0\,\Omega\,°C^{-1}$

7.17 **a** 0.45 m    **b** 2.23 m    **c** 4.5 m

7.18 **a** 0.11 $\Omega$    **b** 4.2 n$\Omega$

7.19 0.14 m$\Omega$

7.20 31 mA

## Chapter 8

8.1 If there were air molecules in the container, the $\alpha$-particles would scatter off them as well and distort the results.

8.2 The mass of the neutron is similar to that of the proton, so neutrons can affect the protons and neutrons in cells quite significantly, through the transfer of energy in collisions.

8.3 **a** 7 **b** 44 **c** 60 **d** 118 **e** 122

8.4 **a** $+e$

   **b** No charge.

   **c** $+Ze$, where $Z$ is the proton number.

   **d** No charge.

   **e** $+2e$

8.5 **a** Proton number = 80 for all.
    Neutron numbers = 116, 118, 119, 120, 121, 122, 124.

   **b** 200.5

8.6 They are grouped into isotopes as follows: $A$ and $E$; $C$; $D$, $F$ and $G$; $B$ and $H$.

   $A = {}^{44}_{20}Ca$    isotope of calcium
   $B = {}^{50}_{23}V$    isotope of vanadium
   $C = {}^{46}_{21}Sc$    isotope of scandium
   $D = {}^{46}_{22}Ti$    isotope of titanium
   $E = {}^{46}_{20}Ca$    isotope of calcium
   $F = {}^{48}_{22}Ti$    isotope of titanium
   $G = {}^{50}_{22}Ti$    isotope of titanium
   $H = {}^{51}_{23}V$    isotope of vanadium

8.7 There are 38 protons and 52 neutrons in the nucleus.

8.8 **a** There are different numbers of neutrons in the nuclei.

   **b** There is the same number of protons in each nucleus.

# Index (Numbers in italics refer to figures.)